BE
unreasonable

paul **lemberg**

BE

unreasonable

THE
UNCONVENTIONAL
WAY TO
EXTRAORDINARY
BUSINESS
RESULTS

McGraw-Hill

New York   Chicago   San Francisco   Lisbon   London
Madrid   Mexico City   Milan   New Delhi   San Juan
Seoul   Singapore   Sydney   Toronto

The McGraw·Hill Companies

1 2 3 4 5 6 7 8 9 0 DOC/DOC 0 9 8 7

ISBN-13: 978-0-07-148163-2
ISBN-10:   0-07-148163-X

McGraw-Hill books are available at special quantity discounts to use as premiums and sales promotions, or for use in corporate training programs. For more information, please write to the Director of Special Sales, Professional Publishing, McGraw-Hill, Two Penn Plaza, New York, NY 10121–2298. Or contact your local bookstore.

This book is printed on acid-free paper.

Library of Congress Cataloging-in-Publication Data

Lemberg, Paul.
    Be unreasonable / by Paul Lemberg. — 1st ed.
        p. cm.
    ISBN 0–07–148163-X (alk. paper)
1. Success in business. I. Title.
    HF5386.L5615 2007
    658.4'09—dc22   2007001180

To my wife, the brilliant painter Leslie Lemberg,
who continues to believe in and support me,
no matter what.
That's what I call unreasonable.

CONTENTS

ACKNOWLEDGMENTS

One unreasonable aspect about writing a book is that it requires you to fix, in one moment of time, ideas that have taken a lifetime or more to develop. I'd like to thank some of the people who have contributed to that development process, and to the realization of those ideas herein:

My mother, Anita Fenson, for teaching me that the conventional and popular way of seeing the world, while not always wrong, is definitely not always right. Without viewing the world through her eyes at an early age, this book would never even have occurred to me.

My friend and book business guru, Mark Levy, for convincing me to do this project; my agent, Jim Levine, for believing in this book; my editor at McGraw Hill, Jeanne Glasser, for helping shape a mass of ideas into a coherent whole; my assistant, Emily Schaerer, for doing her bit to clear the way so this book could actually get done.

For sharing their valuable time, stories, and concepts with me: Paris Arey, Gordon Boronow, Peter Block, Tom Broughton, Tim Carter, Randy Cashingham, Edward de Bono, Fernando Flores, Mike Fry, Steve Harden, Bruno Henry, Tom Johnson, Mark Joyner, Chris Knight, Eben Pagan, Michael Port, Paul Scheele, Jeff Stern, Vernor Vinge, Jeff Walker, and Ralph Whitworth.

A few of the many friends and colleagues with whom I have talked and talked over the years, hashing out ideas and inventing new ones: Tom O'Brien, Paul Myers, Paul Kwiecinski, Bob Serling, Peter Fisher, Kenrick Cleveland, Jay Abraham, Michael Roth, Tom Matzen, Joe Vitale, Rich Gabriele, Khosrow Eghtesadi, Shawn Blair, and David Turk.

As everyone knows, writing a book takes time away from other important things, including one's family, and I especially want to acknowledge my wife, Leslie, for believing in everything I choose to do (or so she tells me) and my children, Kate and Jonathan, for being such great kids.

Thank you all.

INTRODUCTION

Imagine . . .

Imagine that you were free to act, unbound by tradition, convention, history, story, or prejudice. Imagine that you could make choices *simply because they were the right ones*, and not because they fit with someone else's agenda. Imagine decisions being forged in the depths of your clearest vision without being diluted by what you or anyone else thinks you are *supposed* to do. Now, *imagine being guided by your desires rather than your fears.*

What would you ask of yourself? What would you ask of the people who surround you? Would you demand the highest levels of performance? Would you require their best? Would you push beyond your boundaries? Would you dare to attempt your most audacious goals? Would you be unreasonable?

Being *reasonable* is the thing that stops you. Being reasonable is paying heed to that little voice that whispers in your ear and says, "You can't do that. . . . It wouldn't be right. . . . It's never been done before. . . . It's too much. . . . It's too risky. . . . Our customers will think we're crazy. . . . Our people won't stand for it. . . . Our competitors will crush us. . . . There are rules against that."

Being reasonable kills potentially great ideas with arguments about what used to work and what someone else thought made sense at some time deep in the past. Being reasonable is designed for survival. It is about getting by. Being reasonable may keep you in business, but at the same time, it keeps your business from soaring.

Be *unreasonable*, and all those false barriers drop away. The myths that have held you back dissolve, and your inner fire is unleashed. Being unreasonable is a call to embrace your vision, your passion, and your true desires. It is a state of mind, and it is a call to action.

This book is about accelerating your business by having faith in your ability to make the future real. It is about letting go of all the cliché-ridden, time-worn, tired old ideas that keep people small. It is about picking your spot and then stepping out onto the ledge. It is about assessing the situation and leaping into the unknown—not heedlessly, not foolishly, but courageously.

And finding out that you really can fly.

◆　◆　◆

It is difficult to write a *reasonable* book about being *unreasonable*. After all, as soon as an author suggests breaking with conventional wisdom, it begins to seem a bit hypocritical to be enumerating the *rules* for doing so. Mostly, what people want from a book are 10 steps to this or 7 steps to that, and a way to pick all the low-hanging fruit from the tree with little or no personal risk to themselves. Sorry, but this book won't give you that.

There are no formulas for being unreasonable. You cannot tread in the deep furrows plowed by those unreasonable ones who came before you—it just won't work. There are no precise maps to follow to tell you where to go. You can, however, chart your own course, and the world is rich with natural signposts. Like the positions of the stars at night or the smell of salt in the air, they can help you navigate. There are old habits to avoid, and some new thought processes that, if you try them out, will help you develop your own unreasonable point of view. Do that and you can achieve the extraordinary things we all dream about.

For the sake of organization, the pages that follow are divided into chapters, although they are more like groupings of ideas with which you can experiment. Chapter 1 presents the Unreasonable Manifesto: declarations of unreasonable ideas to shake up your thinking and involve you in the spirit of the thing. If you're ready to jump in right away, devour this chapter and make it your own.

Chapter 2 makes the case for being unreasonable; it will help you focus your thoughts on the most important aspects of this journey. It will push you to actually want to be uncomfortable and to embrace change as the best friend your business ever had. It will also help you see that the ideas on which you have relied thus far may be based on a false sense of reality, and that this reality is well worth questioning.

Chapter 3 examines unreasonable strategy, turning many traditional strategic ideas on their heads. Literally. This chapter looks at a number of radical approaches to strategy and gives you some hands-on tools with which to organize your resources and plan your campaigns. The place to start is with the end and the exit. From day one, plan your business based on how you'd like to leave it. Design your efforts from the *back* to the *front* and reduce the risk of taking a wrong turn in getting there. Unreasonable as it seems, start with the presumption that all your ideas are possible and you just have to figure out how to make them work. Remember, guerrilla fighters always win, so beware of the full-frontal approach to anything.

Chapter 4 gets at the heart of the matter: unreasonable thinking. Because being unreasonable requires fresh ideas, this chapter will show you how to free your mind in order to come up with that breakthrough new concept. Chapter 4 examines useful ways to reject compromise, get out of your own way, provoke yourself into some new ideas, turn your old ideas inside out, and create a brain trust so that when your own brain fails you, you can take advantage of others'. You are cautioned to be afraid of the right things, and, finally, to spend some time *not* working as a way of getting the most out of yourself.

No book about business strategy would be complete without a section on its tactical counterpart. Chapter 5 takes a look at some very specific unreasonable tactics that you can apply to your business. Of course, these are not the tried and true but rather the contrary approaches to old issues: spend more, waste more, forget your budgets, price higher, do less, don't diversify. There are tactics for selecting investments and for deliberately making mistakes. And, tactics telling you how to be a *fanatic*.

Chapter 6 presents unreasonable execution. As former American Airlines CEO Robert Crandall said, "About half the job of management is trying to figure out where the company is going to be 5 or 10 years from now; the second half is execution." Execution is the hard part for most executives; unreasonable execution gives you tools to make it easier. These tools were developed knowing that the biggest barriers to effective execution are not know-how and technical expertise, but a lack of communication, planning, senior leadership, commitment, and accountability, and, most importantly, a lack of will and discipline. I'll give you a new bag of unreasonable tricks, like hurry up and wait, slow things down, play both sides of the fence, and hedge your bets. Even leading like a jerk can have powerful benefits. Plus, there are some thinking tools and ways to really put your company's collective brains in action. Surprising as it is, flawless execution doesn't necessarily involve *doing* anything.

Be Unreasonable concludes with some unanswered questions in the unreasonable future. Inventor Alan Kay said, "Don't worry about what anybody else is going to do. . . . The best way to predict the future is to invent it. Really smart people with reasonable funding can do just about anything that doesn't violate too many of Newton's Laws!" The unreasonable futurist can't look at the past and be a trend follower but rather has to invent the future and be a trend *creator*.

BE
unreasonable

CHAPTER 1

AN *UNREASONABLE* MANIFESTO

Businesspeople of the world, now is the time.

Your tried-and-true ways of getting things done are running out of gas; they no longer provide the outcomes you seek. Because your old ways of behaving sometimes appear to work, you think they will work forever. Unhappily, that is just an illusion; it is likely that if they still work at all, it is only for the near term.

Consider this: extraordinary accomplishments begin with extraordinary ideas and find their realization in extraordinary actions. Think about that one word for a minute: *extraordinary*. Break it into its roots and it says *extra* ordinary. Not extra in the sense of "more than," but rather from the Latin *extra*, which means "beyond, outside, superior to" the ordinary. That's what we mean by unreasonable.

Read through the following principles carefully and deeply, perhaps more than once. Use them to find your new truths. Being unreasonable means achieving the extraordinary by doing things that are unexpected, unpredicted, and beyond what normal people consider normal.

Being unreasonable requires rejecting compromises. Compromises force you to sacrifice what truly matters in exchange for efficiency and expediency. They are insubstantial things that exist because of a belief in a false context. Change the context and the compromise dissolves.

Don't wait to play the high cards in your hand. Being unreasonable is about giving your best in every single situation in which your best is called for. It is about asking for excellence in people because it is in everyone's interests. People hold on to their aces, waiting for the right time to use them. Don't hold back. Play your best cards.

Do more than you are asked for. Most people don't ask for what they truly need, and therefore they don't get it from you. Ask people for more than others usually do; you will shock them into action beyond what they thought themselves capable of doing.

Act on the possibility of things. Being unreasonable is about acting on the possibility of great things without worrying about the probability of success. This increases the probability of success dramatically, ensuring that things that are possible become real. Make the improbable happen by bringing attention and resources to those things that lie beyond the norm—beyond the expected—but that can change your world.

Consider why normal is normal. Ask how normal things became that way. Is it because they were effective, or is it because they were easy? Being unreasonable is not about being abnormal, paranormal, or transnormal—it is about looking beneath and behind the normal so that you can see how it got that way, and once you understand why that normal is considered normal, acting to create the results you seek without regard to what *normal* people think.

You know what you should be doing. So do it. You don't need more gurus and pundits to tell you what to do. You have already taken it all into consideration, and though it may seem unreasonable, you already know what to do. Take action.

Think *whatever* thoughts. Reasonable thinking is the silent editor, the censor who disapproves of and redacts your errant thoughts. Think whatever thoughts arise and follow them to their best conclusions. Often the most transformative ideas come spontaneously and unbidden. Then, reasonable thinking kills them. Don't let it do that.

Don't base your life on what's likely. If you have been paying attention to the world, what you now consider likely is already incorporated into your business activity. It is probably also incorporated into your competition's. Search your world—internally and externally—and find the promise of the possible.

Expect the best. Unreasonable as it seems, expect the best from those around you. Expect them to be successful. Count on it. Plan for it. Budget for it. Expecting the best gives you the highest likelihood of getting it. Start with the optimal scenario and truly grasp how to ensure that it happens. Expecting the worst has a similar, but opposite, effect.

Back yourself into a corner so that the only place to go is forward. Warrior-sage Sun Tzu wrote that nothing is as dangerous as an enemy who has been backed into a corner. Such enemies will fight to the death, for they have nowhere else to run. Use this strategy on yourself.

You don't have to do something just because someone says you should. *Should* always implies the status quo. Ask, "Why should I?" whenever the conversation turns to shoulds and shouldn'ts. Should is the road to mediocrity. "Why should I?" is the first step toward majesty.

You can't improve something you don't understand. Don't base your reality on fantasy or falsehood. Many strategies and plans are based on wrong or incomplete assumptions, which necessarily lead you astray. If you don't know accurately where you stand, you can't chart a true course leading from there to your goals.

Plan your exit strategy from day one. Most businesses are built on an idea or an opportunity presented today, with little thought being given to how things will wind up. The result is that they wind up wherever and however they do, often to the dissatisfaction of the leaders. Choose your exit strategy (your final move) today and chart a sure course toward it.

Freedom comes from responsibility. Be completely responsible for your actions and your results. Normal people look for causality, something or someone to blame for the way things turned out. Unreasonably lay claim to every miracle or debacle within your sphere of influence; make them all yours, for that's the only way to exert dominion over them and gain freedom. Being unreasonable is about being totally responsible for everything around you and completely irresponsible about transgressing cultural norms.

You must spend, otherwise you'll go bankrupt. As stated in the Book of Ecclesiastes, there is a time for everything, and so there is a time for thrift and frugality. But cutting expenses to the bone will retard your growth and cause your business to fail. If it is growth you seek, spend more.

You must waste, otherwise you cannot create. How much genuine creation works the first time? If your business shrinks from waste and failure, it will also avoid experimentation and innovation. You must make mistakes if you are to achieve great things. Take action now and empty your trash bin regularly.

A conservative model produces conservative results. Repeating the successes of the past, preserving tradition, and keeping everything the same can at best produce results like those in the past. The problem is that in this new future—our present—those results will not be as good as they once were. Unreasonable success requires unreasonable approaches to the future.

Take Fridays off. Working nonstop (24/7 for 365 or whatever) until your tank is empty is for dullards and plodders. Take Fridays off and refill your tank. Going full steam ahead day after day after day can produce excellent short-term results, but it can also produce exhaustion. Not only physical fatigue, but also exhaustion of the spirit, exhaustion of ideas. You must re-create if you want to keep going. Take time off and use that time to develop new energy.

Don't worry about getting it right. That's what Version 2.0 is for. Perfection prevents progress. New ideas must be tested against real human beings. If you wait to get everything right, it will be very late when you get there. It may even be never. Think functionality and workability. Experiment in the chaos of the market and fix the problems that arise later.

Be afraid. If you're not scared, you're not doing anything worthwhile. All great ventures contain within them an element of risk and the promise of failure as well as success. If you are not at least a little afraid, you are probably not doing anything that will ever be called great. Unreasonable people are often afraid. Just be sure you are afraid of the right thing.

Being unreasonable is about breaking rules, but not about creating new rules. Don't break old rules only to replace them with new ones. When the new rules become simply "the rules," they will bind you just as surely as anything that was there before them. If you must, create signposts, guidelines, and indications. Anything but rules.

◆　◆　◆

There are three meanings of *reasonable*: the reason of logic and common sense, the reason of explanation, and the reason of fairness. Whichever meaning of *reason* comes to mind, being unreasonable is about violating your common presuppositions. Breaking tradition. Contravening the accepted sense of justice. Defying conventions and logic and all the ideas about what has worked before. Any and all of this—at once, if possible.

But make no mistake; this is heady and sometimes difficult stuff. It takes powerful reasons to be unreasonable.

CHAPTER 2

BEING *UNREASONABLE*

"**B**e reasonable!" How many times have you heard that in your life? How many times have you said it yourself? If those admonitions have any meaning at all, why should you do the opposite? For most occasions, being reasonable—acting in the way most people expect—is the right thing to do. But not always.

And thank goodness. This wouldn't be much of a book to read if the subject itself was so unreasonable as not to be worthy of serious consideration. Yet the idea is so important that you must take it very seriously if you are committed to making your business take off from wherever it is right now.

What do you do when the reasonable thing—the expected thing—isn't working the way you planned? What do you do when the reasonable thing—the way you and your peers were taught to behave—isn't getting the results you'd hoped for? What do you do when the things that have worked so well in the past—things that, in fact, are still working—*just aren't working well enough*?

By now you should have figured this out: you become unreasonable. Occasionally you come across an individual who acts in a brash, creative, counterintuitive way, and does it all the time. As a consequence, people like this produce some pretty striking results day after day. But this doesn't describe most people, and it may not describe you.

Most of us act in ways that are acceptable and predictable. We respond within certain boundaries and limitations. We respond reasonably. And most of the time this is OK because reasonable behavior gets us pretty good results. But there are times that call for something beyond OK. They call for a stronger response, a different response—perhaps a response that's so unusual that everything we generally know about getting things done falls short. That's when you need to be unreasonable.

When Things Go Well, We Don't Question

When things are going well, we don't question our everyday actions. Why should we? What we're doing is making our business hum along just as fine as we'd like.

Consider the American car industry, circa 1970. It had a reasonable formula that had worked quite well. Not only Americans, but prosperous car buyers around the world wanted larger and faster cars, and American manufacturers were able to churn them out year after year. They kept buyers buying with lots of model variations, ample chrome trim, and occasional new technology like headlights that dimmed themselves and automatic retracting seat belts, producing sufficient profits year after year to keep shareholders happy. Nobody really worried about foreign car manufacturers that were turning out undersized, underpowered, and no-frills cars—distinctly un-American cars.

Then came the first oil crisis in 1973, and Americans suddenly stopped buying leviathan cars because they couldn't afford the fuel. Japanese cars started grabbing all the headlines; these once marginal producers began stealing market share from General Motors and Ford. They even bankrupted Chrysler.

When things go well, we don't question the accepted wisdom. Americans like large cars. Our recent history reconfirms this, but all it takes is a sharp change in outside circumstances for the reasonable to become unreasonable, and vice versa. All of a sudden, small cars, even tiny cars like the original Honda Civic—first introduced in 1972, ahead of the oil crisis (were the Japanese clairvoyant?)—caused a run on the market, completely reversing 50 years of car-size inflation. This about-face contradicted everything that the entire industry had been raised to expect, and it caught the American manufacturers completely by surprise. How could this happen? Because when things go well, we don't question. We just do what is expected and what has worked for so long.

Let's roll the clock forward a few decades and consider the energy business. Some big energy producers are thinking about the future, and others are—well, we're not sure. The years 2005 and 2006 were banner years for the oil-producing giant Exxon Mobil. When things are going well, most companies don't want to rock their own boat. In late 2005, on the heels of a record $10 billion in quarterly profits, Exxon Mobil announced that it had no plans to invest any of those earnings in developing alternative or renewable energy. "We're an oil and gas company. In times past, when we tried to get into other businesses, we didn't do it well. We'd rather reinvest in what we know," said Exxon spokesman Dave Gardner at the time. Of course, this makes sense, and it's very reasonable, except in the context of an explosive Middle Eastern political climate and a dwindling and increasingly expensive resource.

Compare that to another giant oil company, Chevron. Chevron is thinking seriously about the time when the oil wells will run dry, and it is making plans to produce energy in other ways. This is pretty unreasonable thinking for a company that currently produces most, if not all, of its income from petroleum extraction, refining, and distribution. Chevron is examining a variety of advanced energy technologies and is funding clean energy research. Chevron's experiments range from the somewhat conventional (squeezing more energy out of feedstocks like coal and tar sands) to more radical approaches like fuel from biomass, hydrogen, and even nanotechnology. Chevron's chief technology officer, Don Paul, unreasonably believes that rather than finding more stored energy to mine from the ground, molecular engineering—literally rearranging the sequence of atoms and molecules—is the key to the global energy future.

Whether or not he's ultimately right about this particular approach, the point is that he's thinking along unreasonable lines. While traditional producers like Exxon Mobil see the future through rose-colored glasses and are happily embracing the status quo, former "oil companies" like Chevron, Shell, and Great Britain's BP are considering what must happen if they are to continue to provide energy in a world of rapidly changing political, economic, and environmental conditions. They've chosen to break with their own very successful traditions and find a way, rather than stick their heads in the sand and hope that things don't change too much.

It's difficult to consciously break with the status quo, and it appears that the larger and more entrenched a business is, the harder it is for that business to take actions that are counter to a thought framework grounded in a strong—but possibly false—sense of well-being.

IBM dominated the market for large computers so well and for so long, with each year bringing new meaning to the word *big*. There was just no way that this company would embrace the possibility of small computers. Big was reasonable. Centralized was the only right way to look at things. That point of view controlled not only the company's product philosophy, but also its manufacturing, its selling process, and its own internal corporate structure. This was clearly a case of what's good for the goose serves the gander equally well.

The 1970s trend toward departmental computing, championed by companies like Digital Equipment and Data General, did little to impact IBM's "bigger is better" philosophy; the goliath's response was mostly to make big computers smaller. When microcomputers started to gain inroads, IBM's response was typical. First it tried to marginalize PCs. It kept the products on the sidelines and sold them via separate channels. It tried to preserve its traditional mainframe business instead of realizing that it's "big iron" game was ending and that it was only a matter of time. Had IBM taken the point of view that small computer power could grow and would do so dramatically, it could have led the PC revolution instead of ceding the bulk of the profits to other companies such as Intel, Compaq, and Microsoft.

In the end, IBM was forced to shift its entire business into the services sector, shutting down or selling off various parts of its hardware manufacturing capability. It is when things cease to go well that we are forced to switch gears and look for solutions in unreasonable places. If only we could get ahead of the curve instead.

Breakthroughs Never Happen from Being Reasonable

Incremental improvement—that steady, year after year 7 percent gain in revenues and profits—is based on finding things that could work better and making small changes so that your operations become a bit more efficient or effective. This concept of optimization, set down by W. Edwards Deming, will produce yearly, if small, dividends for your investors. Optimization, or continuous improvement, is always going to be a sound approach to running your business, with a couple of caveats:

As long as the external environment remains stable.
As long as there are no oil price increases or shortages of
    other critical raw materials.
As long as there are no sweeping price reductions.
As long as consumer tastes don't change.
As long as there is no technological shift at the core of your
    product line.
As long as there is no global competitor altering the
    fundamentals of your market.

But when the marketplace is not stable, when great sea changes are tearing at the very fabric of your environment, the only thing that is going to keep you in business is creating a business breakthrough.

A breakthrough is a discontinuous change in your business that shifts the revenue, production, and profit curves in a completely new direction. Breakthroughs—the kind you'll need if you are to compete with a global competitor or deal with a 180-degree swing in consumer tastes—cannot come from "being reasonable" and adhering to your existing business rules. Breakthroughs are not predictable from where you currently are, and they have the nasty habit of making everyone in your organization totally uncomfortable.

In 1983, Intel, now the world's largest semiconductor manufacturer, made most of its money selling semiconductor memory. The company had come under increasing pricing pressure from Japanese manufacturers, who were building significant fabrication capacity while cutting prices to grab market share. Then President Andy Grove concluded that Intel couldn't continue to compete on this basis, and he crafted a radical new approach.

Grove decided that Intel's future—in fact, the future of the American semiconductor industry—lay in microprocessors, which until that time had been a tiny portion of Intel's profits. He refocused the entire company to become a "single source" for computers-on-a-chip, increasing quality and diversifying the company not by product, but by geography, making it a more stable and reliable supplier. He bet the company's future on this breakthrough, broke every rule in the business doing it—and transformed Intel into one of the three most important companies of the personal computer era.

Sometimes breakthroughs happen by accident, yet even when they do, it takes guts to pursue them, because the consequences create tons of discomfort. In addition, they are generally, by definition, totally out of alignment with your current business direction. Moreover, to deliberately set out to engineer a breakthrough from scratch requires a complete sacrifice of everything you hold to be reasonable. So what if profits are down; that doesn't mean you should dump the main profit engine, does it? In Intel's case, it did.

Fortune Cookie Fortune

Mike Fry's Fancy Fortune Cookies is the country's largest manufacturer of the novelty after-meal oracles. It's an unusual business, but it makes perfect sense for Fry, who ran off to join Ringling Brothers and Barnum & Bailey Circus as a clown, and parlayed that experience into his own long-running children's TV show, *Happy's Place*.

If you've ever eaten in a Chinese restaurant, you've eaten a fortune cookie. You know, those beige crescent-shaped cookies with bits of paper and wise-sounding sayings stuffed inside. Mike Fry found his fortune inside of one. Colorless and cardboard-tasting, normal fortune cookies are fun to crack open, but no one would say they are fun to eat. Eating in his favorite Chinese restaurant in 1987, Fry wondered why nobody made a party-colored, good-tasting fortune cookie. Something like a jelly bean. He noodled this idea for a long time and three years later set out to fulfill his dream.

That's when Fry found out that not only didn't anybody make "fun" fortune cookies, nobody was going to. Moreover, they weren't going to let him do it, either. All fortune cookies were manufactured by native Chinese, and no non-Chinese person had ever made them. In fact, the technology for fortune cookie manufacturing was a closely guarded secret, and anyone who sold to the wrong people risked being ostracized by the rest of the fortune cookie community. Fry proposed something that the industry mavens considered not only unreasonable but unconscionable.

After calling every manufacturer he could locate and being rejected by one after another, Fry found someone who was willing to listen. Together they began to experiment. Fry had the good "fortune" to have no idea what he was doing, so he was able to break every rule in the fortune cookie book. He baked "a bazillion" bad cookies before hitting on 17 amazing flavors that his growing customer base loves, along the way inventing the business-to-business fortune cookie market. And without even trying, Fry reinvented the entire ancient art of cookie manufacturing. You can't quite imagine what a fortune cookie machine is like, but Fry and his team of Chinese rocket scientists (yes, his team really has rocket scientists) devised a completely new manufacturing process, using simpler and more reliable machinery than the fortune cookie machines of old. He has defied every single fortune cookie convention—not because he wanted to, but because he had a vision, and the old ways of doing things simply would not deliver.

Breakthroughs are never "reasonable." They can't be, because being reasonable means continuing along the lines of your current business. Reasonable is always moderate, judicious, self-consistent, and rule abiding, all words that imply doing things the way they have always been done. Breakthroughs are the opposite of that. Breakthroughs require rule breaking.

Ctrl-Alt-Delete

There are times when a business model just gets stuck. The old, reliable patterns of product development and business development are producing fewer and fewer returns. It's not possible to say exactly why this happens, except that in a complex environment—like a computer operating system—the combined effects of other players' actions can cause your efforts to get all garbled and twisted.

A year earlier, your latest marketing launch might have made a big splash in the jeans market, but now, because of a new distressed jeans company with a promotional budget as rich as Croesus, your efforts produce nary a ripple, and all your reasonable efforts are down the drain.

So you go back to your trusty playbook, that well-worn collection of tactics and strategies that has always helped in the past—new product models, splashy launches, even a celebrity spokesperson—but nothing seems to work. And worse, you still don't know why. Your new competitors seem to be reaching the market in ways you don't understand at a fundamental level. They're promoting via something called "social networking." What's that, you wonder. They don't even have retail distribution, and yet they're gobbling up all the advertising space. What's happening here?

Relax and take a deep breath, because nothing you know how to do is going to work. Running one of your old plays is just going to dump more money down the drain. It might be time to hit the three-fingered reset command: Ctrl-Alt-Delete.

That's what it's like when you decide that the old rules—the ones you think still apply—aren't giving you what you want. The once reasonable actions of the past are having no effect. Ctrl-Alt-Delete. Unfortunately, hitting the reset keys and choosing to be unreasonable won't make your competitors and their brash thinking go away. But hitting reset gives you the opportunity to dispose of your constraining thought patterns.

Hitting reset is a way to achieve a new level of thinking. Instead of asking a question based on what you know has worked in the past, you can start asking about what—in the realm of possibility—might work now.

You are no longer fettered by previous success; you are free to move into the future. "What is social networking, and how can we get some?" might never have occurred to a company that distributes all of its products through Wal-Mart or Target.

Your decision to be unreasonable clears your mind. As long as you are consumed by making what's not working work, you will keep cycling back to the same limited set of options.

Why do you think most cars look the same each year, no matter who manufactures them? Even when one company introduces something radical, within a single product cycle every carmaker has copied it. And why do you think all car companies use the same basic technology, even though there are significant and evidently superior alternatives available? It is because all the players are locked into the same system of rules, and no single player is willing to go very far outside of those rules.

The evolution of a superior television standard is another example of a situation where the technology that's available commercially lags behind what has long been available in laboratories. The equipment manufacturers, the programmers, the broadcasters, the consumers, and even the journalists and critics all have to agree on a standard. They are all locked, quite reasonably, into a system that is still profitable, although diminishingly so—and no one is willing to take the economic risk of breaking the rules.

These are two examples of systems where the agreements between the players are such that stepping outside those agreements could prove fatal. Does the same hold true in your industry? Are you bound by a consensual set of constraints that limits your ability to address new opportunities? In most businesses, this is not the case. The rules are not rules. They are just accumulations of past history. They are not legitimate market constraints; they are the way you've always done it.

For years, there has been a set pattern in the movie business: limited release to make sure that the film "works," large-chain theater release, rental and retail sales (first VHS and later DVD), video on demand, premium cable, airplane, and finally broadcast networks. This is a system that was worked out by the movie studio executives years ago in the belief that this pattern brings in the greatest revenue by maximizing each layer of "higher-paying customer" before moving on to the next, lower-paying level.

Intuitively, this sequence makes sense. Or does it? Side-by-side comparisons have been difficult, and, until now, no one has ever violated this approach. The exception is "straight to video," which is a special circle of hell reserved for movies that failed to please audiences in their initial screenings, films that everyone "knew" would fail, and specialty genres with limited appeal, like pornography and martial arts.

There are numerous significant problems with this approach, many of which stem from the fact that theater releases are quite expensive and very risky for the producers. Theater owners want proven product on their big screens, which means movie stars and sequels, both of which limit directors' creative options and drive up costs dramatically. Everyone else down the distribution chain depends on the marketing and exposure generated by the theater release. And the theater chains require it, so the system prevails.

Academy Award–winning director/producer Steven Soderbergh implemented an unreasonable approach. Soderbergh, a longtime rule breaker, released his *Bubble* as the first film with near-simultaneous distribution via theater, high-definition television, and DVD. Predictably, the big theater chains boycotted the film, but there were enough independent screens to provide distribution. While ticket sales dropped off immediately, the film was still able to produce profits because both its talent expense and its marketing expense were much lower than normal.

Will this work for mainstream movies? It doesn't have to. Unreasonable is not about changing mass behavior—although ultimately it might. Hitting the reset keys is not going to be the solution to everyone's problems, but it could be the solution to yours.

Will you break the rules that come from your own past behavior, or perhaps (even more boldly) break rules set down by decades of industry norms?

You Already Know What's Most Important

Right now (yes, right now), take out a sheet of paper and write the numbers 1 through 10. Make a list of 10 to-do items, any one of which would help your business substantially. These items can be simple (e.g., "add a new sales team member") or complex (e.g., "split my company in two"). Don't spend a lot of time deliberating about your choices. Just write whatever comes to mind.

Finished?

Now, review your list. Each item is important, but one will stand out. One will make a bigger difference in your life than the others. Don't deliberate here, either. Call upon your intuition, snap judgment, common sense, or whatever you want to call it. Find the most important one and circle it.

Now (yes, right now) begin working on that circled item. Right now? (But I've got other things that I'm working on.) Yes, right now. Dive in. Now.

The thing is, you already know what needs doing. You made a list, looked it over, and decided which item you'd profit from most if you completed it. You don't need additional motivation. The result you achieve from taking action will be reward enough.

We look to complicate life, particularly in business. We can't believe that certain things can be simple. One simple thing is that we already know what to do. We don't need a lot of sophisticated management theory to help us figure things out. We have good answers inside our heads. The trick is getting them out. Sometimes when I do this list-of-10 technique with a consulting client, he'll discover what's most important to him, but he still won't know how to start work on it. At least, that's what he says. I show him otherwise.

Say he decides that his most important item is to increase sales. I ask him to create another list: a "Here's How I Can Increase Sales" list. Only this one won't be 10 items long. It'll be 100 items long. At first, the client thinks I'm joking. I'm not. I give him three hours to make the list. He's going to have to stretch his mind to think up that many items. Some will be simple; others will be complex. Some will be silly; others will be useful. The only rule is that he must come up with 100. Not 87 or 99; 100 is the number.

Why 100? It's a big number, it's as good a number as any, and it's pretty unreasonable. I find that when we have a target to shoot for, even when that target is ambitious, we hit it. When the client finishes his list, we go over it. On a typical list, I'll find 20 strategies that might do the job. I point that out. Here he believed he didn't have even one method, and he's got 20. I get him to pick the strategy that he feels will work best, and I get him to start on that immediately. What I'm accomplishing with these lists is really the consulting world's unreasonable secret: get clients to solve their own problems.

The truth of the matter is that most people already know what to do. They may not realize it, or they may be scared to admit it, but they have the answers. My job is to help clients think clearly, and to get them to discuss their issues with precision. My job is to help them get the possibilities out of their heads and onto paper, where they can act on them. I'm there to clear the junk out of the way so that they can use the knowledge and wisdom that they already had when I got there.

You have this knowledge and wisdom, too. You have good answers at this very moment. Do the unreasonable. Don't pretend you're confused. You know what to do. Do it.

Unreasonable Always Means Uncomfortable

People are tremendously adaptable, but on the other side of every adaptation, we hope for stability. We are creatures of comfort; from a very early age, we find ways of working, and we get used to them. The longer we do something, the more comfortable we get. We quickly lay down rules based on our behaviors.

One of my clients is a serial entrepreneur running a software business. Last year was a tough one for his company. It survived largely by providing add-on services to existing customers—a smart response to difficult circumstances. It worked so well that the company even grew revenues a bit. But here's something else that happened: people got comfortable. They decided that they could exist on their current base of customers, and then they "realized" that there would be no new customers. Is that bad? Isn't that just accepting reality as it is? It might not be bad, except that the team got used to the idea of "no new customers" and stuck with this. The team members believed that it was true and based their whole working regime upon it. Their business development activities dwindled to reflect this new "rule." Now they are looking at an empty pipeline, and unless things change soon, their future will not be bright.

There is a state of mind I'd like to acquaint you with known as the comfort zone. Perhaps you are already familiar with this insidious disposition. People get seduced by the status quo. They think things are pretty good the way they are—no matter what that current state is. It is comfortable. We like it this way, and we don't really want anything to change. When I was a young pup at General Electric, we called this the state of being "fat, dumb, and happy." It gives rise to rules so that we can keep things as they are.

You can become comfortable with all sorts of things—good and bad. You can become comfortable with your existing level of business, even if it is not quite as much business as you'd like. You know how to handle it, you can keep your staff size level, and you know how much profit you can earn from it. Or you can become comfortable with your sources of business, even when your niche is shrinking. After all, you understand these types of customers. You know their personalities. You are familiar with how these particular people will react to your ideas. Isn't this great, you think.

You can become comfortable with your competitors, even if they are bigger or more nimble or just plain better than you. At least you know where you stand, right? And since you think their moves are predictable, you perceive a measure of safety. Remember the old saw, "Better the devil you know than the devil you don't"? Where do you think that came from?

As you can easily see, each of these situations is fraught with danger. If not right now, then soon.

What Is So Comfortable about the Comfort Zone, Anyway?

It goes all the way back to prehistory. Human beings like regularity and predictability. Change is bad. Consider the existence of a hunter-gatherer living life in the wild: every change in the weather, every change in the environment, every new sound in the night, new people, new animals—every one represents a potentially mortal threat.

There are no longer saber-toothed tigers in my town, but we still prefer it when things remain constant and stable. We've learned the right responses to feel adequate to the challenge. We know how to gauge our efforts, and we don't need to work too hard to get acceptable results. And, we can make reliable predictions about the future, which makes us feel safe and secure. The weird part is that we can feel the most comfortable when unknowingly we are in the most danger.

Look at that software company. These people got so used to others saying no to them that they just pretended that this was a good thing and stopped looking for new business. At least it was something they understood, right?

Wrong!

Staying in the comfort zone will kill your business, just as surely as it will kill that of my client. When you are in the comfort zone—that place of pleasurable ease—it means that you have accepted the existing rules and made peace with the status quo. You like it. You hope things are going to remain just the way they are. You aren't changing with the changes. You aren't making progress. You have probably lost sight of your vision, and you are doing things you've done over and over and over . . .

The precipice you are rushing toward is just out of sight around the bend, and sharp rocks are below just waiting to break your fall.

What can you do about these nice-feeling but dire circumstances? It's time to start breaking the rules. You know that's going to be uncomfortable. It always is.

Take this test to see how deep in the zone you really are.

Score 5 points for each yes.

☐ Have you and your team become used to "the way things are"?

☐ Have you stopped pushing the business forward? (Consider any major change as "pushing.")

☐ Have you ceased looking for new opportunities?

☐ Can you think of more than one recent time when you have you taken your eye off the ball?

☐ Have you started to let certain previously important things slide?

☐ Have you become comfortable with your current circumstances?

☐ Do you dislike change?

☐ Have you let your vision become words on a plaque? Has it fallen by the wayside?

☐ Was your last innovation more than one month ago?

☐ Do you know your company could accomplish so much more?

☐ Is everything just fine?

Score 5 points for each *no*.

☐ Can you state, with clarity, what new ground you have taken this week?

☐ Have you contemplated your vision or your mission this week?

☐ Have you scored a major win in the past two weeks?

☐ Can you name two things that you know you don't like, but you've finally gotten used to? Score 5 points for each one.

☐ Can you name two things you have sacrificed for your vision in the past month? Subtract 3 points for each one.

Scoring:

10 or under: You are definitely not in your comfort zone.

11–15: You are straddling the border of your comfort zone. Remind yourself of your current mission. Figure out what hidebound business rules are holding you back and resolve to start breaking them, one by one.

16–20: You are definitely in the comfort zone. Start the five-step program immediately.

21 or more: You are deep in the zone. If you can rouse yourself, seek help quickly—preferably from someone who seems to break rules easily.

Five Steps Guaranteed to Get You Out of the Comfort Zone

Step 1: Recognize That You Are in the Comfort Zone

Have you become used to the way things are? Have you accepted the idea that the way things are is the way they are going to be? Have you stopped pushing your business forward? Have you ceased looking for new opportunities? Have you started to let certain things—important things—slide? Have you become comfortable with your current circumstances?

Step 2: Revisit Your Strategic Goals

What is your business in business for? What goals have you set to help achieve that? Does following your restrictive rules help? Is what you see in your future really what you want?

If you no longer feel strongly about the vision you have, then it's time to do some vision work.

Step 3: Look for What's Holding You Back

What habitual business behavior is keeping you from realizing your vision and corporate goals? In other words, what's not working? These are the rules you were meant to break! Be specific. Be concrete. (You don't need a whole strategic plan here—just get the motor running again.)

Step 4: Examine the Consequences

If you remain in the comfort zone, what is likely to happen next? What are the consequences of maintaining your status quo while the world around you changes? Be brutally honest. If things truly look rosy, wonderful. Good for you. But if they don't . . .

Step 5: Time to Take Action

The stuff that used to work, well it don't work now.

—Warren Zevon

In the end, the only thing that makes a difference is action. Whether you need a shift in what you do or a shift in who you are, either way you need to take action if something is to happen. And you may not be used to action—you may have lost the habit.

Here's a quick solution to bursting out of the comfort zone: set five new actions that will move things forward. Pick one and execute it right away. Start today. When you're done, pick another and do that. And so on. It sounds simple—and it is! The hard part is lifting yourself off the couch and getting started. Things feel so good the way they are, don't they? Getting out of the zone may not be comfortable—in fact, it definitely won't be.

By Any Means Necessary

Important things don't just happen; they have to be made to happen. It doesn't matter whether it's a great invention, a new product launch, or a dramatic increase in market share or annual profits. Or some new safety initiative or a source of nonpolluting electric power. Or world peace.

None of these things happens by itself. They are not the product of circumstances or random events. They take determination, focus, and commitment. They take the actions of someone who has the end result in mind and who believes that the achievement of that end result is dependent on him.

Great things are not achieved by the casual, but only by people who take full responsibility for going out and changing the world—by any means necessary.

Within their system of right and wrong, unreasonable people will do anything they can think of to make turn their dreams into realities. And, of course, most really important things are the product of dreams.

They may have to work 80-hour weeks for weeks on end or create 100 ideas in order to come up with a good one that makes sense. They may mortgage their houses for seed money or even move to places with lower costs of living to stretch their incomes. They will ask customers for help or confront coworkers, even when it's uncomfortable (especially when it's uncomfortable).

In short, they will unreasonably do almost anything to turn their ideas into realities, because that is the only way that important things, great things happen.

Unreasonable people see themselves as stewards of the outcomes they seek—whether it's making a movie for entertainment, challenging a gigantic competitor in the marketplace, or freeing their countries from the bonds of colonial powers.

Brothers Andy and Larry Wachowski, already accomplished screenwriters, sought backing for their big-budget movie *The Matrix*. Despite proven writing credentials, producer after producer turned them down because no big studio would bankroll such an expensive movie with first-time directors. They needed a first film. So they did what any unreasonable young movie directors would do. They quickly wrote the screenplay for *Bound*, a dark, daring, and, most important, low-budget film. *Bound* was cheap to make, and the Wachowskis easily got it funded. It became a critical underground success and led producer Joel Silver to put up $63 million for *The Matrix*.

Act as If Your Life Depended on It

> *Failure is the condiment which gives success its flavor.*
>
> —Truman Capote

Do you think it's unreasonable to take a year and a half making one movie just so that you can make another? What if that's the only way you can reach your dreams? The Wachowskis acted as if their lives depended on it by spending 18 months just to reach another goal.

Acting on the belief that the world needed a reliable source of illumination not dependent on poisonous, flammable gases, the English physicist and early electrician Sir Joseph Wilson Swan produced his first experimental lightbulb in 1860 and spent the next 15 years trying to perfect it.

Building on Swan's and others' successes, Thomas Edison picked up the baton in 1878 and threw the full resources of his laboratory into the effort. Edison worked on the problem for three years before discovering a reliable combination of elements and conditions that allowed his lightbulb to burn first for 13 hours and then for 100 hours before proclaiming victory. "I have not failed. I have just found 10,000 ways that won't work!" Edison reportedly said while being hounded by a journalist. While the 10,000 may have been hyperbole, it indicates the depth of commitment and unreasonable ends to which Edison was willing to go.

Goals of significance—and lighting a benighted world certainly counts as significant—require people to act as if their very lives depend on the outcome. Ultimately, Edison said, "Many of life's failures are people who did not realize how close they were to success when they gave up." If your life depended on it, how far would you go? How many no's would you endure? How much failure?

Film star Mark Ruffalo washed dishes, planted trees, painted houses, and tended bar in Los Angeles while he endured eight years of rejection, reportedly getting turned down for over 800 parts before landing a role in a major movie. Jack London received more than 600 rejection slips from magazine publishers before he sold his first short story. John Grisham, author of books selling more than 60 million copies, was turned down by 15 publishers and 30 agents, and 123 publishers rejected Jack Canfield and Mark Victor Hansen's *Chicken Soup for the Soul* before it went on to be one of the best-selling books of all time. More reasonable people would quit long before reaching success.

Laurence J. Peter, author of the eponymous *The Peter Principle*, believes that "there are two kinds of failures: those who thought and never did, and those who did and never thought."

While Peter meant something else entirely, he is expressing a perfectly unreasonable sentiment. Unreasonable people "do" without considering the cost of "doing." When your life depends on it, the cost doesn't matter, does it?

Internet marketing pioneer Mark Joyner told me this unreasonable story about his early days in the military.

I was working in military intelligence and was recommended by my battalion commander to attend Officer Candidate School. Generally, when you're selected by the battalion commander, that pretty much means you're going to get in because that commander is putting his reputation and career on the line by recommending you. That notwithstanding, you have to go through a vast number of red-tape hurdles, which in retrospect seem as if they're actually there to see if you have what it takes to go through them. If you can't navigate your way through that bureaucracy, you'll never make it, because as an officer you have to deal with a ton of it and a whole lot worse.

So I started making the rounds to the various agencies on the post—Camp Humphreys in the town of Anjung-ri in South Korea. It's just like any other American Army base, and I'd drive from place to place, agency to agency, getting various bits of this paperwork checked off. But everywhere I went, the guy in charge would tell me, for one reason or another, I was either ineligible to go to OCS, or, and I'm not sure how this is different, I simply could not go.

The first time this happened, I had gone to pick up the original paperwork, the Battalion S1—who's really the manager of paperwork—the paper-jockey there told me flatly, "You can't go to OCS." I said, "I think I can—can you just give me the paperwork?" So he shoots back, "I'm not going to give it to you—because you just, well you just can't go." This got me going, so I said, "I don't mean to make any trouble, but that's not your decision. Just give me the paperwork."

This kept happening, and I went through this same story again and again and again. I stopped counting the thirty-seventh time I heard the word "no." I don't know how many times it happened after that, but I finally got to attend OCS, despite the fact that every one of these people said NO to me.

Each time, I had to be more and more unreasonable to these folks, who each claimed with perfect authority that I couldn't, and wouldn't, go. In cases like these, being unreasonable is not only a good idea, it's essential for your survival. I hadn't thought about being unreasonable; I just acted the only way possible.

It's Your Responsibility

Unreasonable people see themselves acting as if things are their responsibility. If they don't do it, who will make sure it happens? Swan and Edison acted as if bringing cheap, safe nighttime light to the world was their responsibility. American patriots like Samuel Adams and Paul Revere repeatedly risked execution in resisting the British Crown and what they considered "intolerable acts." They saw it as their responsibility. Nelson Mandela endured 27 years of harsh imprisonment because he would not abandon his dream of a free South Africa. He was offered release in exchange for renouncing armed struggle, but he would not abandon his principles or his people or his responsibility. Marie and Pierre Curie unwittingly sacrificed their health, and ultimately their lives, to understand the secrets of radioactivity. They knew how important it would be for saving other people's lives, and they saw it as their responsibility.

Perhaps this sentiment is easy to understand when you are fighting for freedom. The 1960s Black nationalist Malcolm X said in a famous speech:

> We declare our right on this earth to be a human being, to be respected as a human being, to be given the rights of a human being in this society, on this earth, in this day, which we intend to bring into existence *by any means necessary*.

Even in a business context, a sense of personal responsibility can drive people to act in a way that "normal people" will consider unreasonable.

It is often said that great salespeople don't take rejection personally. It's just business, it's not you, right? That's just nonsense;

of course it is you. But it doesn't matter who it is—if it's your responsibility to get the sale, you just keep going. If it's your responsibility to bring in the revenues and the profits and keep your company going, you do whatever it takes.

Normal, unassuming businesspeople routinely put their homes, their futures, and even their families at risk for the sake of their business ventures. And while we hear a great deal about the 62 percent of all American businesses that fail, there are no statistics on the risks that business owners take in order to keep their companies' doors open and keep their employees working.

Aaron Feuerstein became a national hero and a role model for corporate responsibility because of the decisions he made while standing by the smoldering ruins of his Massachusetts textile factory. Unreasonably, he spontaneously vowed to rebuild Malden Mills on the very same site—even though other locations made more economic sense. He even continued to pay his employees their wages and benefits during the rebuilding effort. His actions saved hundreds of jobs in the community and fostered both employee and brand loyalty unequaled in the textile industry. (We find it unreasonably odd that *feuer* is the German word for fire.)

Betting the Farm

Leaders like Nelson Mandela, the Curies, Sam Adams, and Paul Revere saw accomplishing their visions as their personal responsibility, and they willingly put their lives at stake. Aaron Feuerstein bet his company to support his unreasonable sense of responsibility. Thousands of entrepreneurs routinely bet the mortgages on their homes and the futures of their families because they hold it as a responsibility. After all, if not they, then who will strive for the goals from which a better world is built?

Creation is an act of courage and responsibility. Are you willing to "bet the farm" on your ideas? Is your vision that clear, your goals that compelling? Your very willingness to risk everything can, all by itself, inspire others to greatness.

No More Bad Days

It's reasonable to assume that you should be happy when things are going your way and miserable (or at least unhappy) when they're not. After all, happiness is a reaction to the circumstances of the moment, and if the events of a particular day make you unhappy, then that day is a bad one.

Celebrated dog trainer Barbara Woodhouse had a wildly popular book called *No Bad Dogs*. Her premise was that there are no bad dogs, just bad owners with bad training methods. Likewise, there are no good dogs, just good owners with good training methods. Woodhouse believed that the dogs themselves were neutral, neither good nor bad.

Unreasonable as it may seem, in much the same way, there are no intrinsically bad days. Days themselves are neither good nor bad; they are simply 24 hours of pure potential, and they are colored either good or bad by the attitudes of the people that inhabit them. You have 24 hours to forward your business in any way you can imagine, if only you can remain focused on your intended outcome.

If you decide that you're going to be happy and pragmatic, productive and effective, no matter what, you'll be better able to deal with any day's unique changes in fortune. Perhaps it's unreasonable to think that every day can be "good" because the consensus is that days actually have ups and downs, a mix of "high" time and other time. There are external circumstances, outside forces at work—aren't there?

No, not if you've chosen to be responsible for how your day goes, there aren't. George Bernard Shaw said it eloquently in his play *Mrs. Warren's Profession*: "People are always blaming their circumstances for what they are. I don't believe in circumstances. The people who get on in this world are the people who get up and look for the circumstances they want, and, if they can't find them, make them."

Deciding that this will be a "good" day, that it will go well and be productive, forward-moving, and powerful—that you will gain new customers, make more money, and build your business, irrespective of "the day" itself—that's the unreasonable point of view. Once you've decided to bet the farm, it only makes sense to further decide that you have neither the need nor the time to have bad days.

Viktor Frankl, author of *Man's Search for Meaning*, was a medical doctor and psychotherapist who spent the years 1942 to 1945 in Nazi concentration camps, including Auschwitz. Frankl not only survived the subhuman brutality of the camps but also maintained his sanity and sense of well-being while watching many of his fellow prisoners die, all the while wondering how his survival was possible. Frankl concluded that man could prosper and flourish, no matter what his circumstances, as long as he had a personal sense of meaning and purpose.

"The one thing you can't take away from me is the way I choose to respond to what you do to me. The last of one's freedoms is to choose one's attitude in any given circumstance," Frankl wrote. In the end, it all comes down to attitude, and the unreasonable attitude is that things can and will go your way. Frankl shows us the way to never have another bad day. Meaning. Purpose. Goals. And a belief in your power to choose.

Reasonable Is Often a Fantasy

Microsoft chairman Bill Gates is widely quoted as saying, "People always overestimate what's going to happen in the short term, and underestimate what happens in the long term." We think Gates is correct, and we wonder why people are such conservative forecasters when it comes to their own work.

Entrepreneurial businesspeople tend to be quite optimistic about their own abilities to get things done. They tend to plan in a vacuum, and thus ignore the possible effects of external forces, unintended consequences, and the random influences of chaos that arise from any complex project. As a result, when making personal forecasts about what they can achieve in the next month or year, reality consistently falls short of their forecast when the deadline comes due. In short, they overestimate, giving us one aspect of the fantasy. This kind of optimism can get quite out of hand. There's even a tongue-in-cheek formula used to tune forecasts from software developers that isn't too far from the mark: take a programmer's estimate and cut the number he gives you in half, but move up to the next unit of measurement. For instance, when a programmer tells you it will take four days to complete a project, make that two weeks. If she says it's six weeks, convert it to three months.

Over time, businesspeople do learn from their experiences. They learn that no matter what, they never quite achieve their forecasts, and that the world, represented by their teachers when they are young and bosses or investors when they get older, penalizes them for it. Being basically intelligent, they rein in their forecasts and become conservative. This is the pessimistic part of the fantasy. Either way, whether they are openly optimistic or conservative, it's all made up—none of it is based in reality.

Let's look at the future aspect. Gates is correct in saying that we underestimate the future. Why? Another complex and paradoxical answer. For 50 years we've heard forecasts from futurists and scientists about impending breakthroughs that will revolutionize our lives, but our short-term experience proves that reality never quite matches up with the forecasts. So over time we discount the forecasts, particularly the more dramatic ones, and ultimately don't believe that any of what is predicted is going to happen.

But the forecasts do eventually come true—just not in the time frame originally stated. Jules Verne's rocket ships did come true, only it took a half century longer than expected. The twenty-first century wristwatch communicator is now much better than Dick Tracy's ever was—Tracy's didn't have GPS built in. Laptop, and even palmtop, computers give everyday users powers that no computer scientists even hoped for 30 years ago, and medical advances like DNA screening for killer diseases, surgery without sharp knives, and artificial, custom-grown organs—all forecasts of 1960s science fiction, have started to become available. They're just late, that's all.

Here we have many different aspects of forecasting—short and long term, conservative and optimistic—and each of them is based on a fantasy analysis that is only partly grounded in real, objective information. These forecasts are repeated endlessly, day in and day out, until they are seared into the corporate or the collective consciousness. They become "reality." They become "reasonable."

The source of ideas and information that we call "reasonable" is often people's cover-their-butt understatement of potential or a conservative estimate of industry progress, but either way, it is mostly based on old wives' tales and off-the-mark groupthink. Ideas that we daily call reasonable are often based on fiction, not fact. This means that you have to get a better grip on things—you have to understand the real business reality.

The 10 Percent Solution

> *Twenty years and $40 billion. They seem like good round numbers.*
>
> —Michael Dell, founder of Dell Computer

When I was in business school, we were taught, quite seriously, that when you needed an estimate of a rate (for anything), 10 percent was a safe number to use. Not because there was any scientific or statistical foundation for it, but because people would almost always accept 10 percent as reasonable. No one would challenge you. Never mind if the 10 percent wildly overstated or seriously understated your results—your calculations would have the ring of authenticity about them, and your reports would be accepted. This was career counseling, not advice on accuracy.

Over time, I have seen people use 10 percent for estimation when they've had no business doing so; I do it myself all the time. You need a number—any number will do, so why not use one that won't raise eyebrows? The only problem is that it's total fiction, and any conclusions drawn from it are similarly fiction. You're just as well off plucking the answer out of thin air.

Lies, Damn Lies, and Statistics

Many people, in attempting to ground themselves in reality, turn to one of the great sources of its opposite: statistics from the media. Let's clear something up. All media outlets, whether conservative or liberal, left or right wing, social commentary or business commentary, share the same business model: get people reading their publications and expose them, early and often, to advertisers. Once you accept this as true, everything else about the media starts to seem false. Fact checkers at the most respected publications accept low standards of proof, and the evidence of veracity is usually quite thin. For the most part, it's all good, clean fun, except when you are using reported "statistics" for your business decisions.

I'm not sure what Mark Twain was referring to when he wrote about "lies, damn lies, and statistics," but his point was clear. You can make seemingly factual data support any argument you like, if you massage them properly. You can leave outlying numbers "out" or put them in. You can use averages, means, medians, or modes. You can use a chi-square, Bayesian, normal, or any other kind of distribution. And if none of these things works, you can change your interview questions. Or your sample size. Or switch among multiple choice, true or false, and fill in the blanks. You can select aided or unaided recall. You can use random sampling or a panel of respondents. You can even use disproportionate stratified random sampling to make your case. And if you're not happy with any of these, you can always find an expert to provide an opinion.

You may not know precisely what these things mean, but you should get the point. The statistics from the popular media that you rely on are just as much a fantasy as your own forecast of your company's next 12 months' performance.

Earlier in my career I worked for a market research and strategy firm and was discussing project parameters with an executive from a client, a large computer manufacturer. The outcome of the project was predetermined: my client wanted data to support what was already a foregone conclusion. Sample size? Methodology?

These were mere details. What mattered was a cogent set of statistics that could be used to strengthen his recommendation to senior management. Statistics can make your case, or they can break your case. They can be used to substantiate almost any argument you care to make.

This is not meant to be an argument against statistics, just a recommendation that you exercise caution when interpreting them and be aware of their origin. And you should never, ever, base your conclusions about what is reasonable and what isn't on someone else's rundown of the prevailing reality.

Benchmarks

Long ago, when more things like tables were made of wood, a carpenter would mark the length of an object on any free edge of his workbench, making a tick with some sharp object. He did this so that the next piece—say the next table leg—would be the same length. This became known as a benchmark. Now we use the term *benchmark* to mean an objective reference standard against which to measure performance.

Benchmarking *seems* like a good idea, especially when your company wants to set a new performance level and isn't sure what that level should be. Often we turn to a known benchmark, like a competitor's performance or an industry average, and benchmark against that. And that too seems reasonable.

Except that it isn't. First, even if the data are accurate—which they often aren't—they are taken out of context. We might know how much money our competitor is spending for marketing and benchmark against that, but without understanding its sales compensation program or the rest of its cost structure. We might benchmark against an industry-derived revenue-per-employee number, but not know the capital expenditure needed to support it.

Second, the benchmark itself may be just plain false. Just like statistics gleaned from the media, industry benchmarks are often published to promote a particular agenda, and competitors' benchmarks may even be disinformation. Imagine that.

Use the same caution when approaching external benchmarks as you do when considering media statistics. They can be valuable guidelines for formulating your own business plans, but they are just as likely to be reasonable-seeming nonsense that will lead your business down a garden path lined with rattlesnakes.

Unreasonable Does Not Mean Unrealistic

Being unreasonable does not mean being unrealistic. It does not mean basing your business in fantasy. Instead, it works best when you are grounded in reality.

If you're going to base your business on something new, it's helpful to truly understand what has gone before. If you're going to base your business on what's possible, you need a way of understanding what's possible. If you think that 73 percent annual growth is possible because that's the industry average, it helps to know if that is really true. Too many bad business decisions have been supported by false, misleading, or even ridiculous data.

Several years ago, a software developer client planned to segue into a niche market adjacent to the one it already controlled. On one level, the move made sense, as the two markets utilized similar production technology and required a similar approach to data management. I asked the management team what the company hoped to gain from doing this. They regaled me with all sorts of numbers regarding the size of the market, the demographic distribution by revenues, and the large underserved portion—all of whom they hoped to gain as customers. They had gotten their information from speaking to an "industry expert," who had gotten the information (supposedly) from "industry sources." It all seemed pretty reasonable, except that I doubted their assessments. I ended up acquiring some U.S. Census Bureau information on the client's behalf to get the official count of how many companies of what size there were in this market.

Thank goodness I did, because it turned out that the client had overestimated the market size by a factor of 4! This ill-conceived move would have ruined the company. Talk about reasonable.

Best Practices Aren't

There is one more source of apparent reasonableness that leads companies to make disastrous decisions: best practices. Best practices are based on the unreal notion that a method that is effective for one successful company will be equally effective for another and will lead to the same success. Of course, that assumption does not take into account differences in staffing, skill sets, underlying products and technology, distribution networks, relationship with and loyalty of customer base, capital base, and hundreds of other variables.

In fact, there is almost nothing to support the concept of best practices, except as a point of information or as a point of departure for your own thinking. Best practices are as ridiculous as the notion that one size fits all. It doesn't, and it never will. Of course, there are general guidelines for what is right and wrong in an industry, and the list of what has worked for others may be something with which to familiarize yourself. But best practices? As a guide, maybe. As a prescription, definitely not.

Why Being Unreasonable Is the Most "Reasonable" Thing You Can Be

The reasonable man adapts himself to the world; the unreasonable one persists in trying to adapt the world to himself. Therefore all progress depends on the unreasonable man.

—George Bernard Shaw

What is called reasonable—doing what others have done before, following the norms, aligning yourself with the conventional wisdom, basing your decisions on available statistics, all in an attempt to produce great business results—may be the craziest thing that you can possibly do. In your quest for stellar profits and brilliant outcomes, being reasonable is most likely going to lead you to mediocrity. How could being reasonable do anything other than revert your results to the mean when your decisions are guided by the lowest common denominator—either yours or someone else's?

Instead, act unreasonably. It may be the only "reasonable" thing to do. Find new ways to think, ways that are beyond the bounds of normalcy, outside the common wisdom, and perhaps even offensive to the crowned heads in your company. Unreasonable thinking must always take you outside the realm of the common.

But be careful; unreasonable does not mean idiotic. Being unreasonable is no guarantee of success, and a bad unreasonable idea could take you in the downward direction just as easily as in the upward one. But once your ideas make sense—which means that you think they have a strong shot at working better and getting you what you want—they don't have to make sense in terms of history; they just have to make sense now.

Develop a concrete sense of reality—yours, not someone else's—and base your actions on that. Develop a concrete sense of "now-ness" and use that to determine what makes sense right now. Do what needs to be done for its own sake, not to satisfy some strictures placed on your operations by what was decided long ago.

Now that you've decided that it's OK to be unreasonable, you're going to have to figure out how to approach things. Once you've decided to leap off the bridge, you want to make sure that the water is deep enough and that there's a way to get back onshore somewhere downstream. That's where strategy comes into play. The purpose of strategy is to select and arrange your resources in a way that will give you the best possible outcome and achieve your vision.

CHAPTER 3

UNREASONABLE STRATEGY

Why Is Strategy Important?

Being unreasonable is doing what is unexpected and unpredictable, and going beyond what is normal. Most people either think of strategy as "the big plan" or use the word as a synonym for a way of doing things.

To unreasonable people, strategy is neither of these things. Unreasonable strategists know that things change without reason, and that since most people act irrationally, you can't really predict what they're going to do. Economists like to talk about efficient markets and perfect information; this means that everybody knows everything all at once, and that since people are rational, you can predict the choices they are going to make. That's really a nice idea, but it bears little relation to reality.

Markets are chaotic, competitors are sneaky and duplicitous, consumers are undereducated and irrational, and the whole environment is surrounded by a fog of disinformation known as promotion, publicity, and advertising. There is an investment theory called random walk that says that the past movement of stock prices cannot be used to predict the future prices. Random walk can be applied to the market players as well. Since we are not mind readers, we have no idea what anyone is going to do. Not really.

Von Moltke's Dictum

The nineteenth-century Prussian general Helmuth von Moltke said, "No battle plan survives first contact with the enemy," and he was right. Von Moltke was talking about the famous "fog of war." During a battle, smoke from cannon and rifle fire obscured a commander's view of the battlefield, and the general chaos made it very hard to understand anything beyond the present moment. More importantly, von Moltke understood that the enemy he was fighting was not some static thing, but a group of responsive human beings whose actions he could not predict with any great certainty. He knew that battle plans had to be fluid and plastic. In the space of an hour or a day, new tactics would have to be substituted for old, and the whole arrangement of forces might need to be resculpted.

You cannot know what is going to happen, but since you are not ignorant and have some experience with the players—or at least you think you do—you make educated guesses. That is the basis of strategy. Because things are highly likely to change once it all gets going, the unreasonable definition of strategy is

Selecting and arranging your potentially scarce resources to best achieve your most important objectives.

This definition presupposes a few things.

First, it presupposes that some resources are scarce, and for most of us they are. Time is often scarce—and by scarce I mean that you could use more of it than you have. For many business-people, money is scarce. Whether it's in your budget or your bank account, you generally would like to spend more than you have available. People with the right skills are often scarce. For some companies, customers are scarce. Raw materials can be scarce. As you can see, scarcity, even for those of us with "unlimited resources," is a way of life.

Second, it presupposes that you have real, important objectives, but then anyone who is reading a book like this, one that promises unreasonable solutions, probably has big things to accomplish; things so big that he can't get them done the easy way.

Third, it presupposes that there is something out there—whether it's a competitor, an "enemy" of some kind, or perhaps something more abstract like a goal or a vision—that you want to conquer. It further presupposes that your objective or opponent is more powerful than you and might even have access to unlimited—or at least more abundant—resources.

Guerrilla fighters present the clearest example of strategy in action, which is why Jay Conrad Levinson, author of *Guerrilla Marketing*, chose that name for his small business approach to marketing. Guerrilla fighters battle against a larger, richer, better-equipped enemy. Because they themselves are ill equipped, they have developed methods of combat that avoid direct confrontation and make maximum use of the limited food, weapons, ammunition, and technology that they have at hand.

Guerrilla fighting stresses deception and ambush rather than mass confrontation, just as guerrilla marketing stresses direct marketing tactics, one-to-one marketing, and word of mouth over advertising and broadcast promotion. Guerrillas succeed best in irregular, rugged terrain—much like niche markets. They employ hit-and-run skirmishes instead of sustained battles—like their business counterparts who execute a single time-limited campaign and evaluate the results. Each of these guerrilla approaches exemplifies positioning resources, putting them in action, understanding the outcome, and repositioning them for the next engagement.

There is something else important to note about guerrilla strategy. While we often do not agree with their philosophy, aims, or goals, guerrilla fighters are in every case inspired by a sense of possibility. They have compelling personal reasons to fight. They fight not for salary, or as a result of conscription, but because of a sense of purpose. They fight for what they believe is a better way of life or a better future for their families. They are often trying to defend their right to run their own countries; some are even trying to change the world.

This is a very important thing to consider, because in the history of warfare,

Guerrilla fighters always win.

Possibility or Probability

Strategy is defined as selecting and arranging your potentially scarce resources to best achieve your most important objectives. So the first step is to figure out what those objectives are. In setting your strategic objectives, you can consider the world in terms of what opportunities are available and what is likely to happen, or you can decide what you think might be possible for you to accomplish in the world, and then look for ways to make that happen. This leads to two different approaches to crafting your business strategy:

- Strategy from the Outside In, or the Strategy of Probability
- Strategy from the Inside Out, or the Strategy of Possibility

Strategy from the Outside In

Traditional business strategy is Strategy from the Outside In. The key tool that traditional businesses use to aid this kind of thinking is called SWOT. Pronounced "swat," this acronym stands for strengths, weaknesses, opportunities, and threats.

The SWOT process is based on examining two large sets of factors. The first is made up of the environment in which you operate, including customers in the market, competitors, regulators, availability of materials, the state of technology, and so on. By themselves or in combination, these factors offer opportunities to be taken advantage of and threats to be avoided. The other set of factors is your internal situation—your strengths and weaknesses—including your cash in the bank, your existing customers, your market position, the skills your staff possesses, your intellectual property, your system and processes, and so on.

By matching the opportunities and threats that you perceive in the external environment with the strengths and weaknesses that you see in your internal situation, you are able to come up with a set of strategies to capitalize on the opportunities or mitigate the threats.

SWOT works, and when properly carried out, it can help you get the greatest return on your resources. Also, because SWOT is a systematic way of looking at your world, you may see opportunities on which you can capitalize. It is a very reasonable way to organize your resources.

SWOT gives you a set of strategies based on what is probable. By definition, it looks at what already exists, and it enables you to take the best advantage of things that are already in play.

Strategy from the Inside Out

The other way to craft strategy is by creating it from the Inside Out. This is what I call the Strategy of Possibility. This approach is based not on opportunities you glean from studying the market but rather on your organization's vision, purpose, goals, and dreams. It asks the fundamental question, "What are you trying to accomplish in the world?"

What does your company see as a possibility that *needs* to be realized? The Strategy of Possibility begins with this question as a starting point and proceeds from there. It succeeds so well because people who embrace it have a compulsion to make something happen.

The Strategy of Possibility is about unreasonably betting the farm to bring something important, either personally important or globally important, into the world. Of course, you still have to make choices about how to secure and apply your resources. But you do it from a different perspective—one of inspiration rather than observation.

SWOT strategy is past-based. It seeks to capitalize on the company's previous successes, all the things leading up to the current state of affairs. And, yes, it works, but it rarely produces anything spectacular. It is a mental structure that is designed to promote conservation and incrementalism. It has to be that way, because it is often about repeating the past, taking advantage of the current situation, and repairing failing mechanisms.

There is nothing wrong with incrementalism, and companies that rack up 5 to 15 percent profit gains year after year can achieve stability and large returns for their owners. This much is true, but there always comes a time when the previously successful approaches begin to fail. Over the course of years, they produce smaller and ultimately negative returns. In fast-paced markets, the time to failure can be short indeed. Try competing against Google.

Taking another look at the American auto industry in the early 1970s, we find the well-developed, highly profitable business structure that actually invented the SWOT concept. Year after year, this industry refined its business approach, one tweak here and another there, with annually expanding profits. At one time, the auto industry *was* American industry. There was even a slogan, "What's good for General Motors is good for the U.S.A." That was true until the first oil shock, followed by the rapid incursion of Asian car imports. The U.S. car industry has never recovered; it has continually shrunk in market share, workforce, and profits, while possibility thinkers like Soichiro Honda and Kiichiro Toyoda rapidly expanded theirs.

The Strategy of Possibility takes as its starting point your company's purpose and vision, and establishes a set of measurable goals. In some happy cases, these goals will mesh with opportunities that are already apparent in the market, in society, or in technology, because that is how we as human beings think.

Have you ever noticed that Hollywood tends to release two or three movies on the same subject simultaneously? Or that, working independently, two or three scientists around the world will publish within days or weeks of each other experimental results addressing nearly the same problems? This may be coincidence, or it may be what psychiatrist and philosopher Carl Jung termed synchronicity.

We tend to visualize and set as our purpose goals that are already part of the collective unconscious. At the same time, opportunities tend to appear before us that weren't quite visible previously. That doesn't mean that they were not there; it just means that we couldn't see them, in large part because we weren't looking for them.

You Don't Know What You Don't Know

When you don't know that something even exists, you don't know that you don't know it. This may sound silly at first, but it bears consideration:

You don't know what you don't know.

If you're not aware of something, you don't know that you don't know anything about it. If you don't know that you are seeking something, not only do you not know what to look for, but you don't even know to look. You can't ask the right questions about something you don't know is possible. You don't even know that there are questions to ask!

So, of course, you can't see the opportunities, because even if you are looking straight at them, you don't recognize them as such. Opportunities are like viruses—except in a good way. Viruses have receptors that allow them to attach to cells that have the opposite receptors. And just as a square peg cannot fit into a round hole, a virus with the wrong receptor cannot attach to a cell that doesn't match. But in the virus's case, it doesn't even "see" the mismatching host cell; it is attracted only to the ones that fit.

So it is with opportunities. When an organization has expressed a clear, compelling vision and purpose, it can start to become aware of opportunities in the marketplace that were previously invisible. Once you know about something, you can begin to know more. Entire worlds become available. And once you decide that this thing, vision, or purpose has become your destiny, all sorts of things stand out in high relief, making themselves known to you to use to your advantage. It starts to feel as if things are placed there just for your convenience by Adam Smith's "invisible hand."

William Hutchinson Murray, author of *The Scottish Himalayan Expedition*, sought to climb the Himalayas as part of an expedition that some friends were assembling. Recently graduated from Oxford, he didn't have the funds to travel, and he felt instead that he should be looking for a job. His friends continued to badger him, and for months he waffled—should he stay or should he go? As Murray tells it, there came a moment when he realized that in his heart he was an adventurer, and that this trip was the path to his destiny. He decided to go, putting it this way:

> Until one is committed, there is hesitancy, the chance to draw back, always ineffectiveness. Concerning all acts of initiative (and creation), there is one elementary truth the ignorance of which kills countless ideas and splendid plans: that the moment one definitely commits oneself, then providence moves too. A whole stream of events issues from the decision, raising in one's favor all manner of unforeseen incidents, meetings and material assistance, which no man could have dreamt would have come his way.

Murray's experience, although poetic, is not unique. It can happen this way for you. Your vision can become so clear that the path to its attainment jumps right out at you, as when the runway lights up at night for a pilot coming in for a landing.

But not always. For most businesspeople, breakthroughs happen in the mind's eye first, long before anything else. The end is like crystal, but the path to getting there is as clear as mud. The only thing that is known is that there must be a way, and they will find it.

If There Was a Way...

Many business owners lament, "There's just no way to . . . ," and they let that one little phrase stop them. For years, in our Business Acceleration practice, we've been telling clients,

> "Yes, I know there's no way to do that. But if there was a way, what would it be?"

In fact, there is always a way, but if you shut down your thinking with a can't-win point of view, you'll never see it. By taking the unreasonable perspective: "But if there was a way, what would it be?" you can begin to discover or invent that way.

Possibility Strategists presume that there is always a way; they just don't yet know what it is. There are always opportunities to be discovered, resources to be acquired, ideas waiting to pop into their heads. It just hasn't happened yet. By establishing a lucid vision and purpose, along with a set of goals for their realization, a company's attention is focused on finding those things that are necessary to make it happen.

Don't mistake this for a Pollyanna point of view. We are not expecting that the world will be good to you just because you want something badly. Rather, we believe in a point of view that suggests that the world is rich with opportunities, resources, ideas, and people willing to participate. Your good ideas can inspire others to act, gathering to you and your cause, as Murray says, "all manner of unforeseen incidents, meetings and material assistance, which no man could have dreamt would have come his way."

Possibility Strategists, people like Apple's Steve Jobs, Microsoft's Bill Gates, and Sony founder Akio Morita, start with the idea and an assumption that such things—whatever they are—are possible. Then, and only then, do they set teams to work figuring out how to make them happen.

Akio Morita, one of Sony Corporation's two founders, had a goal of overtaking the Western electronics industry. This is an example of an Inside Out goal if there ever was one, and it certainly wasn't based on any SWOT analysis saying that it was likely. Bill Gates expressed his vision like this: "A computer on every desk and in every home," which was not at all in line with the fabulously expensive computers of the middle 1970s. Steve Jobs and his partner Steve Wozniak started with a question: "What do I want the computer to be?" They were certainly not looking out in the marketplace for answers to their question. Later, after the Apple II had taken off, they asked, "Why should human beings have to memorize anything?" which led to a quest for what became known as the GUI, or graphical user interface, which providence presented to them in the form of Xerox Palo Alto Research Center's user interface for the Xerox Star, which was then adapted by Apple.

Sometimes the tools needed to fulfill an Inside Out strategy already exist. Sometimes they have yet to be invented. No matter; the vision and goals of Inside Out Strategy propel your organization to find them. This is the source of breakthroughs.

Breakthroughs Are Based on an Overriding Purpose or Sense of Mission

Of course, breakthroughs can happen by accident. You can stumble over an opportunity that swings the fortunes of your company in a new direction. Discoveries can happen in the laboratory, demands can change in the market, and events can occur on the global stage, any one of which can present itself to you all wrapped up with a neat bow, just waiting for you to take advantage of it.

Right?

Well, um, yes—and it happens every day, and it may even be just the thing you were seeking.

But the true breakthroughs—those discontinuous, disruptive changes that enable you to leapfrog competitors and transform your business seemingly overnight—don't happen without some kind of preparation. And that preparation requires choosing the path.

IBM was developing a desktop computer after having been goaded into it by many small manufacturers, and Microsoft had control of an operating system that could make it possible for everyone to use this computer. While not everyone agrees, this was a match made in heaven. Bill Gates persuaded IBM to license Microsoft's DOS operating system for its personal computer in a way that was tremendously advantageous to Microsoft's future. Because the license was nonexclusive, Microsoft was able to allow other manufacturers to use the operating system as well. But that opportunity—as unlikely as it may seem, for IBM could have balked and refused the deal—was completely aligned with Gates's Inside Out strategy. Gates drove hard for the terms of his deal because he had a vision to realize, and the agreement with IBM, while colossally important, was only part of the picture.

On a smaller scale, a client of mine who owned a small publishing company had an Inside Out vision to sell his company for $20 million. Over the course of three years, he pursued opportunities of various types with modest success but without the dramatic rise in value necessary to reach his goal. At one point, I suggested that a reverse merger with a publicly traded company would let him take advantage of the Internet boom without going through a time-consuming public stock offering. Almost overnight, the perfect target company appeared, and a deal was quickly consummated. There were some early difficulties, but within 12 months of the deal, my client was able to sell his shares in the company and reach his goals.

Strategy from the Inside Out, the Strategy of Possibility, starts you thinking about how to make "it" happen, even though you begin down the path not knowing. The first step is to convert "I don't know" into "I don't know yet," followed by, "But I will." This transformation allows you to succeed. Without it, you will not.

Developing your business strategy based on your company's values, vision, and goals enables you to put pieces in place on the presumption that everything will be available to you when you need it. This enables you to tune your attention and lock on to opportunities that will further your goals, and tune out things that will not.

Think of this as the red car syndrome. Buy a red car, and you see red cars everywhere. Buy a blue convertible instead, and you suddenly see those. Recently my family purchased a brand-new model car, a fresh and exciting design. It was the first one I'd seen, and I (foolishly) believed that we had the only one in town. On the third day we had ours, I saw two of them, one of which was the same color. Now, of course, I see them everywhere. While there probably are more than there were when we first bought it, the real reason I notice them is that I have one. My brain is programmed with it. I have an emotional connection with the car itself, and I see these cars where previously I would not have noticed them.

Set your sights on finding solutions to a specific problem or ways to realize your company's expansion goals, and "all manner of unforeseen incidents, meetings and material assistance" suddenly become visible.

You are still finding opportunities out in the world. The difference is this: rather than seeing an opportunity and latching on to it because you think your business can capitalize on it—the Outside In way—you decide what it is you want to accomplish. Then you go out into the world looking for ways to make it happen.

That's the unreasonable path.

Why is this so powerful? When you are simply following things that seem like good ideas, you are inclined to abandon them when you meet obstacles. When the going gets tough, those once attractive ideas don't seem as bright and shiny as they previously did. But when your business is built upon a vision, you, your team, and your stakeholders—everybody—are more motivated to take risks, to take action, to seek beyond the obvious, to abandon old, tired routines—all the things that will propel your business forward and enable you to skip over obstacles and leapfrog competitors. To create breakthroughs.

Tom Broughton has spent his entire career in Birmingham, Alabama, banking, and in 2005 he launched ServisFirst. This bank calls itself an *urban bank*, which is a bit of a paradox: community bank personal service combined with big bank products and technology. Broughton has a reputation for unreasonable service, which he solidified as cofounder and president of First Commercial Bank. When he set out to create ServisFirst, he used that reputation to craft a unique and unreasonable funding strategy. Lots of folks wanted to invest in his new bank, but there were conditions. "We were only going to sell stock to people who banked with us," says Broughton. To qualify to invest in ServisFirst, you also had to make deposits of at least seven times the amount of money you wanted to invest. This was unheard of. People were outraged and told Broughton that he couldn't do it—*it just wasn't done that way here*. He says, "It was not common, and to many people it didn't feel good. In the South here, we're always so polite. They felt it was a bit too bold."

But that's what unreasonable people do: they do things that aren't done "that way." And they know that great results don't come from yielding to others' concerns about the ordinary and the regular. But Broughton described his strategy in a way that was less confrontational, and he started calling the bank a cooperative bank. "That's a great word in the world . . . *cooperate*," Broughton says. "Any product or service can be positioned in a way that makes people do something in exchange, and we just called that something cooperating."

It turned out that investors were willing to cooperate. They wanted to put their money with Broughton; eventually they yielded to his demands, and money poured in. The strategy has paid off handsomely. Records set include opening ServisFirst Bank with the highest initial capitalization of any bank ever formed in the state of Alabama, and its growth has been the fastest in Alabama banking history: 10 times its size in asset holdings since its formation. Not only that, but it takes a typical bank two to three years to become profitable, sometimes longer. Because of this funding strategy, ServisFirst was profitable within six months.

Not to rest on the success of one good idea, Broughton and his team have implemented a follow-on strategy whereby you can't even be a customer of his bank unless you are willing to make it your primary bank. The argument goes as follows: ServisFirst takes its name seriously; its mission is to provide superlative service. But it can provide this high-quality service only to customers with whom it has a high-quality relationship, which means a primary banking relationship. So those are the only customers it will serve. Broughton goes on to say, "We will only do business on our terms, and through that we've created a sense of scarcity, something that you can't often do with a bank. If you can give the appearance of scarcity, you can have extraordinary profit margins. It's allowed us to transform a commodity into a relationship."

Seeing the End at the Beginning: The Merlin Method

Once you set a strategy from the Inside Out, your next step is to figure out how to bring it into reality.

The reasonable approach that most people use is to start at the beginning and proceed toward the end. This can work, but not if you don't know what you are doing. How will you know where to start and which step to take next? People who think this way create plans that are tough to execute and that don't really make any sense.

The unreasonable approach to business planning begins at the end and works its way forward. This method is sometimes called Endpoint Visualization. I call it, much less technically, the Merlin Method.

This is the same Merlin, the legendary wizard, who plays a pivotal role in the stories of Camelot and King Arthur, which were based on a fifth-century Briton warlord. One of the more fanciful legends surrounding Merlin is that he started his life as an old man and lived it growing younger. This made him a wonderful soothsayer, because the things that were in "the future" were actually in Merlin's past.

This approach is named after Merlin because it helps you formulate an action plan by looking at the end of things first. Merlin is used to create a plan working from the end point to the beginning. The Merlin Method works by allowing you to "see" the results of your Strategy of Possibility. This is easy to do because you have already allowed the possibility of this strategy—you know that it can be made to happen, even if you don't know how to do it. Begin by visualizing the end of a long process timeline, at some point out in the future, when the end results of this Strategy of Possibility have been achieved. What kind of effect will the strategy have? What products will there be? How many clients will you have? What share of the market will be yours? What will it mean for your positioning? What will it mean for your company relative to your competitors? What effect will it have on your market value or on your share price?

Ask the questions that you consider relevant to this particular possibility. There is no set list; the idea is to make the whole thing more real, to get into the mindset of accomplishing your strategy and also to start you thinking about the path for getting there.

Here are a few more interesting "mindset" questions:

- What skills were necessary to implement this strategy?
- Where did your company acquire these skills?
- What do you believe about your company once you've arrived there?
- What do you believe about your market once you've reached that goal?
- What could this be the launching point for?
- How will you know when you've reached this goal?

Then begin to work your way from the end to the beginning. It's a simple process that's best done with someone else, or perhaps the whole team. Make the conclusion—the desired result—your final milestone on the timeline. Now remember the last significant thing you did *just before* this point. (You'd remember what happened immediately before you were successful, wouldn't you?) What actions were taken? What resources did you need for this step: any tools, materials, forms, information, and people?

Then ask another question: "And what would have to have happened just before that?" For each answer, consider how you got there. What are the details, what decisions needed to be made, what kind of staff or team made it happen, what resources needed to be available, what skills had to be present to accomplish that step or phase of the plan?

Continue rewinding as if you were watching a videotape of the entire process from finish to start. Freeze each frame as necessary and jot down each step. Keep going, asking each time, "And what would have to have happened just before that?" Each significant result has a key action that preceded it, and each key action has a result that preceded it. Build your plan one step at a time, backward, from the future until now. Keep moving backward until you reach the present and the very first step.

When you are finished, put your mental video player on forward and review the process from beginning to end. Play it forward and watch your plan unfold. This doesn't mean that it's perfect; unreasonable plans rarely are. But it is a plan that will put you on the path to reaching your goals.

One of my clients was a sleepy but profitable company selling specialized records management software to the federal government. The owners were pulling out nice profits year after year, but they were bored and had decided that it was time to sell the business. The only problem was that although the business was profitable, the owners could sell it for only a modest three-year multiple of those profits, as it was neither sexy nor fast growing. We began a Merlin Method process with the senior team and developed a scenario whereby the company repositioned itself into two fast-growing market niches with significant market share gains. In the team members' collective mind's eye, the company was now a sexy takeover target.

The team worked its way from the end to the beginning. It developed a fully fleshed-out plan to redeploy the profits into a powerful marketing and sales campaign going after specialized clients and delivering a more focused product and service. It even renamed the product to separate it from the generic tools for which the company was previously known. Reinvigorated, the entire staff jumped in, and within nine months—far short of the projected timeline—the company received and accepted a tender far in excess of the investment banker's original valuation.

Setting your strategy from the future may seem unreasonable. It may even seem like a flight of fantasy for people who portray themselves as hard-nosed and grounded in "the facts." But the real fact is that reasonably playing out the same old line, searching for concrete opportunities that you can see today, here and now, will as often as not lead to subpar returns and lowball valuations.

Following Merlin's lead and looking backward from the future has a solid chance of driving your company to great heights.

Why Does Backward Thinking Work?

Edward de Bono, creativity expert and author of the much-praised *Lateral Thinking*, explains our Merlin Method this way: it is grounded in the principle of asymmetric systems. Think of a tree from trunk to leaf. Now think of the same tree from leaf to trunk. See how these two are different in your mind? That's an asymmetric system. It works like this: the main problem with "normal," front to back, beginning to end, problem to solution thinking is that one ends up taking many sidetracks, which are oh so easy to get into and very hard to get out of. And for the most part, those sidetracks don't yield anything of value. But if you go the other way, back to front, the path is very linear and logical. Think again of a tree. The tree branches, then the branches branch, and so on. If you have an ant on the trunk of the tree, what are the chances of the ant's finding its way to a specific leaf? With every branch, the chance is diminished by 1 divided by the number of branches. The average tree gives the average ant a chance of 1 in 8,000—not very good odds of finding a solution to your problem or a strategy that produces desired results. But what if you start the ant on a leaf—any leaf. Now what are the chances of its getting to the trunk? Much better; in fact, the odds are 1 out of 1, or 100 percent. There are no side trips to take, no false branches. By the way, this is also the explanation of humor, de Bono says. Once you make the mental leap, the explanation is obvious and unequivocal—and you can't imagine it turning out any other way. But at the beginning of the joke, the end is unimaginable; humor is an asymmetric system. And so is Merlin.

Something Worth Accomplishing

The next step in this unreasonable path is to give up "percentage-point" goal setting and to establish objectives that are worthy of your company's pursuit.

Whenever I get a call from someone who wants to hire my firm for help in accelerating her business, the first thing I want to know is what exactly the company is trying to accomplish. If it has meager goals, there's no point hiring us. Even if it reaches them, the meager goals will never be satisfying. Not to management, not to the rank and file, and not to the owners or investors.

People have meager goals because they are limited by their experiences. They believe that they can accomplish only A and B, because in the past they've accomplished only A and B. Beliefs like that become self-fulfilling prophecies. These people automatically apply the brakes once they've reached their self-proclaimed limits.

If someone anchors himself to the notion, "I'm only as good as what I've already done," then he'll have a hard time doing better. He'll achieve only as much as he thinks he can, and that might be far, far less than what he can actually achieve.

The old saw about elephant training illustrates this point. Take a baby elephant and tie her to a stake on a short but stout rope. All she can do is wander within a small circle. Once this has gone on long enough, you can take away the rope, because the young elephant never stops perceiving the rope's hold on her.

People are the same way, except that, being smarter than elephants, they learn much more quickly. Smart people can learn things from as little as a single repetition, which means that even one failed experience can keep them chained to that puny stake for life. Talk about fixed thinking! Business owners' and managers' heads are filled with "factual" stories arguing for their and their companies' limitations and how those limitations play out year after year.

To help a business rise above its fixed thinking, I've got to start people's imaginations cooking and get them to look at what's possible as opposed to what's likely. I put this question to them: "Do you want to play the game?"

Coming up with worthy goals—goals that draw you to them—is a game. Goals like those don't just exist. They're not just lying there, waiting for you to collect them like shells on a beach. You have to make up worthy goals. You have to invent them—sometimes out of thin air.

Let's take the owner of a modest $1 million business. Ask this owner what she wants and she'll usually say something like, "to grow faster." I ask what she *really* wants. Often, the answer is more money. What's the most money she's ever made in a year? Perhaps she'll hang her head and say, "I've only been able to make $200,000." Of course, $200,000 isn't chump change. That amount would put her in the top 1 percent of money earners in the entire world. But, if at one point this woman considered earning $2 million a year, and she's never come close and doesn't believe that she'll ever come close, she'll feel ashamed. You would, too. For good or bad, our expectations rule us, right along with our sense of limits. If she wants her yearly income to grow, she's got to change her thinking. Why? Because $200,000 is as far as her current thoughts have brought her. If she wants to make $2 million a year, we've got to get her thinking $2 million thoughts, which lead her to take $2 million actions. We've got to push.

The Other 10 Percent Solution

What sometimes stops people here is what I call a 10 percent mentality. That is, they think in terms of small, measured gains. Thinking like that usually comes from working in corporations.

There, most employees can't get a raise of more than 10 percent, and often get far less, no matter how good a job they do. Thus, 10 percent becomes a ceiling that employees apply, not only to their salaries, but to their lives.

Instead of coming up with an idea that would increase their department's efficiency by 8,000 percent, they come up with an idea that would increase its efficiency by 10 percent, or 5 percent, or 1 percent. These small increases seem reasonable, and nobody gets in trouble for suggesting them. A giant increase would seem unreasonable. Since they're reasonable people, they don't even go there.

I worked with a midsized company that began in the same year as a much larger corporate giant that shared the same market. The corporate giant is a Global 100 company; my client's revenues are around half a billion. Although it has had some banner years—you don't get to $500 million without some banner years—all of this company's strategic decisions are based on meeting modest growth goals and satisfying current customers' needs. It has never looked out to the future to ask what could be possible. It has never asked, "What is it we want?" and "How could we . . . ?"

Let me be clear: this company has generated a tremendous fortune for the original owners and investors, but as a public company, it has never been a high flyer, and the stock price has recently taken a beating because of its conservatism. It has the 10 percent mentality in spades.

Last year I began to work with a new vice president to help shake up things outside the core business. We've been preaching the message of being unreasonable. Now, for the first time, people are asking these questions. The company has set growth goals far in excess of its track record, and it has allocated some resources to growing its noncore business and laying claim to its share of a rapidly expanding market.

There's a lot of support for the 10 percent mentality. It's ingrained in our culture. I mentioned earlier that I was taught in business school that if you needed a number you didn't have, use 10 percent.

Use 10 percent?

Why not 100 percent? Why not 1,000 percent? Because 10 percent is safe; 10 percent is believable; 10 percent is doable.

Yes, 10 percent is reasonable, and, as I said earlier, we're taught it in business school. This is the number that both Jewish and Christian scripture set as the correct amount for giving, or tithing. The Hebrew and Greek words for *tithe* mean "tenth," or 10 percent. In fact, 10 percent is widely regarded as a reasonable benchmark for everything from strength improvement to weight loss to savings. It has the added support that we have 10 fingers and 10 toes. (Don't discount this part of the argument.) And 10 percent is estimated to be the average profit portion of the entire U.S. gross domestic product, which means that if you add up everything that everyone in the economy, winners and losers, receives, it will net to 10 percent annual gains.

So if you need a somewhat arbitrary number on which to hang your hat, 10 percent is a pretty solid number, isn't it? But this 10 percent takes into account the fact that according to data from the U.S. Small Business Administration, about two out of every three companies with employees go out of business within six years. Do you want to be part of that crowd?

But let's continue for a moment: 10 percent gains, year after year, will double the size of your company every seven years. At first blush this doesn't sound too bad, but there are two major problems with this kind of thinking. The first is that most people fall short of their goals—which is how they fell into the trained elephant thinking trap in the first place. So if your company shoots for 10 percent, what are you really going to achieve? Will it be 7 percent? With that compounded year after year, it will take you 10 years to double your business. What about 5 percent? You don't want to know how long that will take to double (14 years!). Think you can keep it up for that long?

The second problem with incrementalism is that it assumes that the rest of the market isn't changing faster. Your competitors are growing. Your customers' preferences are evolving. And any company that sets its growth sights this low is probably not planning on a lot of fast-paced change. While you are racking up those 10 percent gains, your competitors are crushing you.

So, while, on the surface the incremental approach seems like a safe bet, it is really anything but. Over time, it will lead to failure if it's not mixed in with a breakthrough every now and then.

Much better than the 10 percent mentality is what I'd call Times–10 Thinking. You take what you think is reasonable, and you multiply it by 10, or by some other measure that's just as grand. So, if $200,000 seems reasonable, Times–10 Thinking makes it $2 million. If reasonable is controlling 5 percent of the market, Times–10 Thinking is controlling half the market. If reasonable is getting on the cover of the *Newark Star-Ledger*, Times–10 Thinking is getting on the cover of something far more prestigious, like *The Economist* or the *Wall Street Journal*.

Times–10 Thinking is unreasonable, and it is guaranteed to shake up everything. As soon as you subscribe to this kind of goal setting, the very next words out of your (or someone's) mouth will be, "But we don't know how to do that." Or worse, "We can't do that. It's never been done." But of course it has, just not by you. Of course it can be done; you just have to figure out how. Times–10 Thinking supports the Strategy of Possibility. And liberal application of the Merlin Method will help you develop a possible path to getting there.

In this era of rapid, world-flattening, discontinuous change and global competition, what you think is "normal" just isn't going to stay normal any longer. And what you consider to be "reasonable" is a surefire formula for failure. It may have worked in the past, when change took place over years and an international legal contract had to be on paper and circle the world by steamship. But that's not the case anymore.

People must violate what they think is normal because, as we have seen, normal is always going to fall short. What seems reasonable isn't. What seems normal won't be for very long. And in a fast-moving market, 10 percent growth in anything is likely, over time, to end up looking like a net loss. Times–10 Thinking is the only way to stay in the game.

◆　◆　◆

Let's get back to my mythical client. Now, this lady may be a hard case. She may find it too difficult to think in leaps and bounds. If so, I try a different tack—a smaller, gentler one.

I say, "When you wake up in the morning, what's the first thing you think about?"

"I wonder if the weather will be nice," she'll say.

"And, for you, what's the best possible weather?"

"Warm. Sunny. Maybe 80 degrees."

"Good. Now, thinking about a fantastic future is no more difficult than thinking about the weather. The same way you think, 'I sure hope it's warm, sunny, and 80 degrees today,' you think ahead a year and say, 'I sure hope X happens, Y happens, and Z happens.' The only difference between the weather and making X, Y, and Z happen is that the weather happens by itself. With X, Y, and Z, you'll have to work to bring those about. You embody the result."

If she laughs, I know she gets it. She realizes that dreaming and finding worthy goals aren't hard. They're actually enjoyable. Finding a direction doesn't have to be some grim exercise. It's based on preference. It's based on spirit. It's based on joy.

Stop establishing goals based on what you think is likely. And don't worry about failure. Unless yours is a public company, no one is going to punish you for falling short of your goals. Take to heart the old expression, "Shoot for the stars, and settle for the treetops." If you aim for the treetops, you're likely to fall flat on the pavement.

Make your goals take you to a future that will inspire you to bold action. Base them on your company's vision, your core purpose, your mission. Build an unreasonable strategy based on the future and figure out how to get there. Do the unreasonable: Forget about what's likely. Base your future on what you dream about.

In the End, Tactics Are Meaningless

Many organizations consider it reasonable to stick with a plan once it has been established, no matter what. Even if the plan isn't working, some very reasonable people consider changing course in midstream a sign of failure. Plans are considered sacred, and it is an indicator of strong leadership, they say, to have sufficient foresight to know what will work and what will not. These companies are focusing on the "how" of getting something accomplished rather than on the "what" and the "why." They are making the classic mistake of considering tactics and plans to be paramount, as opposed to pursuing a vision and its outcomes.

Screenwriter William Goldman, writer of *Butch Cassidy and the Sundance Kid* and *The Princess Bride*, opened his bestselling book *Adventures in the Screen Trade* with the important phrase "Nobody knows anything." Goldman was discussing the film business and how its executives, the "suits," picked winners. And how did they do it? By using the same stars, directors, writers, period settings, and possibly even the same subjects, as were in their last hits. Then they try to use the same stories and plots. This explains how there can be two or three vampire movies or volcano movies or poison-snake movies or evil magician movies or time-travel movies all at the same time. When one executive hears that another has just bought a "fish-out-of-water" story, she rushes to find one for herself. It also explains why there are so many sequels and remakes—even prequels. These executives are focusing on the how, in this case the stars, the directors, and so on. They have forgotten the classic definition framed by Earl Nightingale, 1950s radio personality and author of *The Strangest Secret*: "Success is the progressive realization of a worthy idea."

The unreasonable approach to strategy says nothing about how to get there. It says everything about purpose, principles, and outcomes, rather than the tactics you use. Tactics are the "how." According to *Webster's New American Dictionary*, tactics are "a procedure or set of maneuvers engaged in to achieve an end, an aim or a goal." They are not the goal, and yet many entrepreneurs treat them as if they were.

"I need a new direct mail campaign," you explain. No, you don't; you need more leads. "We need fresh, exciting advertising." No, you don't; you need to improve your presence in the market and achieve name recognition to reduce your selling cycle. "We need to acquire our competitors." No, you don't; you need to find a way to dominate your market segment and acquire new technology for the future.

In each of these cases, the tactic has preceded the strategic aim, and in each case, that is simply wrong. It might be right, but not necessarily. Consider a manager whose company indeed does need greater market presence and name recognition, and who decides that the way to get this is through more exciting advertising and so proceeds down that road. But wait a minute—the current advertising was working; it was generating qualified business leads. Too bad, because the new, "exciting" advertising doesn't—it's too creative and too abstract. Nor does it shorten the sales cycle, so the advertising agency is sent back to the drawing board, while other possible promotional ideas, like a PR campaign or targeted white papers, aren't even considered. For many people, tactics rule, because they are easy to get your hands around.

Tactics are meaningless in the sense that a hammer is meaningless. What has meaning is building the new house, not the tool you used to build it. Imagine showing some friends your beautiful new four-bedroom home on two splendid acres, with a swimming pool that has a vanishing edge and a five-mile view. "Yes, we had this house built with a 16-oz. Stanley hammer," you tell them. Actually, you never mention the hammer, do you? Nor do you tell them how the foundation was poured. You may even leave out the part where you began building the house with one crew but had to fire that crew because it didn't show up on time. You didn't keep using that crew just because it was the first crew you picked, did you? You didn't feel compelled to go the distance with that bad concrete for the foundation either, did you?

This may sound silly, but that's exactly how people treat their tactics and their plans. They stay with them because they started with them. They embrace their tactics as if those tactics had intrinsic meaning for the business. This is not to say that tactics aren't important. Of course they are; some tactics are supposed to be more cost-effective and others more affordable, given your budget constraints. Some tactics are supposed to be fast-acting, while others are reputed to show results that mature over time. The key is "supposed to." When you apply them, you find out. If what is supposed to be true about these tactics is true, you keep going.

But tactics can't be true in the abstract. They have to be true for you, and they have to be producing the desired results. If they aren't, you have to change your approach, and quickly. If you aren't reaching your goals, it's not because they're bad goals, it's because your tactics aren't working.

People talk in terms of working harder versus working smarter, and it's important to figure out which to do when. Sometimes the tactic is working, and all that's needed is more of it. More focus during the workday, more hours on the job, more people on the job. That's working harder. But when the tactics don't work no matter how hard you work them, something else is called for—and fast. This is where the idea of working smarter comes in. Working smarter simply means finding things that, in fact, work.

If you're having problems reaching a goal, it might be because you're sticking with a tactic that no longer works. Many sales firms, for instance, still use cold calling as their primary method of prospecting, although new laws are shrinking the practice's effectiveness. Rather than showing allegiance to a tactic, even one that has worked for you many times in the past, it's best to keep your eye on your goal (e.g., to increase sales by 15 percent) and see what fresh tactics might help you hit it.

Tactics and the Comfort Zone

One of my clients called me in to help stabilize his company at a point when it looked like the entire market was collapsing. This was right after September 11, and the management team was running scared. Nothing that had previously worked was working any longer, and the team was desperate—desperate enough to consider throwing in the towel but willing to give it one last shot. All tactics were completely up for grabs; the only things that remained intact were the company's core values and its seemingly quixotic goal of doubling revenues. First we redefined the company's view of the perfect client. From there the company shifted its product positioning to appeal to those clients and crafted a new financing structure that addressed the market's increasingly poor profit picture. At this point, the management team was so far out of its comfort zone that it could barely breathe. Lastly, it revamped the company's marketing program from top to bottom, fired its outside marketing team, created a set of sizzling marketing material designed to appeal to the new client picture, and developed several new (well, new for them) approaches to getting it into prospects' hands, including conducting mini-seminars and using FedEx to deliver direct marketing appeals. Revenues didn't double that year, but within three years, profits were up 400 percent.

Be like this client, and get far—very far—outside your comfort zone. This may not be necessary when your business is humming along, but it is definitely necessary when it is not. Then get out of the comfort zone and be willing to change those tactics that aren't producing for you.

Nimbleness Is a Virtue

It's not your tactics that need a long time to work, it's your strategies.

Being flexible is at the core of bringing your strategies to fruition. While some people deride this as spinelessness and worry about what Wall Street or the investors will think, we applaud it as nimble. You have to be willing to assess the situation and turn on a dime when you are sure that your tactics aren't working. In fact, the ability to change quickly—to substitute one tactic for another, or even one strategy for another when necessary—is a cornerstone of success in the twenty-first century. Keep the good for as long as it's working but immediately ditch everything that isn't good. Tactics. Machines. People. Clients. Everything.

Know How It Will End from the Beginning: Crafting Your Exit Strategy

P. T. Barnum, the nineteenth-century showman, owned a lower Manhattan dime museum. There he displayed oddities, including wax figures, mummies, totem poles, a two-headed calf, and the famed "Fiji Mermaid"—a stuffed creature that was half fish, half monkey. Each exhibit seemed more remarkable than the last.

Down one corridor in the museum stood an ominous-looking door with a sign hanging above it that read, "This Way to the Egress."

You can imagine the patrons' anticipation: "Egress? What's an egress? Is it a bird as big as a horse? Is it a native in a loincloth? Whatever it is, I've got to see it!" When they pushed through the door, they were surprised all right; they found themselves standing in the street! The great Barnum had hoaxed them. The word *egress* comes from the Latin word for "exit," and they had been tricked into leaving the building.

Now, I'm not sure I like Barnum's idea of tricking people into leaving. But what I do like—no, make that love—is his idea of making an exit into something of an attraction. Exits should draw you to them, especially if you're a business owner. Let me explain. If you own a company, you should know how you're going to leave that company as soon as possible. I'm not talking about physical exits. I'm talking about exit strategies.

You might think it weird to include how to leave the business in a chapter on business strategy. It has been said by some of the best minds in history that the surest way to reach your goals is to first know what they are. It's another application of the

Merlin Method. And in the spirit of beginning with the end in mind, it is crucial that you have a concept of how you're going to finish the thing you are now starting.

Even if you're just launching your business—even if you've only been in business for a day—you should have an exit strategy, and that strategy should be as clearly defined and as exciting as Barnum's famous "egress." An exciting exit strategy acts as your business's guiding light. It keeps your biggest payoff clearly in view. It guides your day-to-day actions. If you have an exit strategy that drives you, all you have to ask yourself is this question: "Is what I'm doing leading me toward the exit I want, or away from it?" If what you're doing is leading you toward it, you act. If what you're doing is leading you away from it, you change what you're doing.

An example. One of my clients owned a software business worth $2 million, which he wanted to sell. What made it tougher was that he wanted the business to be worth 10 times that amount within three short years. We unreasonably decided to find the very best possible acquirer—the one that would benefit the most from his company—and craft the business for that acquirer. The first thing we did was to study his marketplace and look for public companies that would receive a substantial increase in stock value from being in my client's market. Then we did a thorough examination of his business, looking at his product development process, sales procedure, company positioning, revenue model, and so on. As we examined each piece, we asked, "Does this contribute to a business that big, or does it detract from it?" If it contributed, great. If it detracted, we figured out ways to improve it. Once we knew the companies that might be interested and the improvements the client had to make, we put all that information into a plan, which included listing the ways my client could get on the radar of the public companies. He started to work on the plan. He worked hard.

In three years, though, he pulled it off. One of the companies he had targeted bought his, making his share of the company worth the money he was looking for. My client cashed out.

Now, you might think what I just wrote about is crass. It's all about money, money, money. In all this talk about cashing in on an exit strategy, where does developing good products and services fit in? My answer: that's up to you, but know that you probably won't realize the value you seek without them.

If developing a leading-edge company is part of your exit strategy, then make it one of your design parameters. Just be certain that you define exactly what "leading edge" looks like. Will you control the market? Will you be on the cover of three industry magazines within six months? Will certain gurus proclaim you "the next thing"?

I pick monetary gains because they're easier to measure than praise. What's more, if you cash out with the cash you want, you can use those funds to bankroll the next company you want to start. I'm a serial entrepreneur, so for me, that's important.

The whole concept of "exit strategy" can be broken down into a few categories:

- Sell your business to another business or group of investors.
- Go public and relinquish the burden of ownership.
- Transform the business into a cash cow and run it until you die.
- Duplicate it, as in licensing or franchising, and extract much of the wealth in advance.
- Give it to someone else, like a child, a relative, or a highly valued employee.
- Just shut it down.

There are surely others, but this little list includes the bulk of them.

Let's face reality: no matter what you plan now, when the time comes to exit, you may think differently. We all know that most plans never reach their end states. These are guidelines, but they are critical to how you structure your business. Each of these exit strategies requires you to create a certain kind of structure, follow a certain path, and take certain steps in order to achieve the end you have in mind.

The first step in any strategy is to define your goals and objectives, and your exit strategy is your *ultimate* objective.

Make Your Own Exit Strategy

Remember, no matter what anyone else tells you, it's never too early to have such a strategy. Even if you plan on owning your company for 40 years, a clearly defined exit strategy can only help you. To make your own exit strategy, complete the following statements. That'll give you a great start.

1. My exit strategy is _____.
2. This year my company will grow _____.
3. Within 18 months we will _____.
4. If I sold the business today, it would be because _____.
5. The company is now worth _____.
6. If I sold it today, my personal net would be _____.
7. My personal net would be twice as much if _____.
8. One thing my company is really missing is _____.
9. My biggest concern, which may keep me from getting there, is _____.
10. My company's financial statements are (check one): audited, compiled, reviewed, other (explain).
11. We have available (check all that apply): forecasted financial statements, recast financial statements, prior three years' financial statements.
12. Name your banker, your corporate attorney, your tax/estate planner, and your accountant.
13. If today a buyer expressed interest in your business, name three intermediaries or investment bankers you could contact to explore the possible merger or acquisition of your company.
14. Name the three companies, or types of companies, that would be most likely to be interested in buying your business.
15. Today, my company has (check all that apply): a written business plan, a written annual budget, written contracts with customers and suppliers, a written manual of employee and company policies, a written manual of its productivity systems, a written exit plan.

Do the unreasonable: run your business by knowing how you want to leave it. Begin it at the end, and you'll have a clearer sense of how you want to get there.

People worry about the how when they should worry about their commitment.

Author Peter Block says that people's tendency to figure it all out up front is really a wish for safety and predictability. They worry about whether something is possible rather than about whether it's worth doing. Once you've chosen to go forward, Block suggests, there is a period of anxiety, a continual nagging worry that would not be present if you'd taken a tried-and-true approach. That's a good thing. Be worried. Be anxious. Be scared.

A friend of mine relates a story about how he precipitously decided to quit his comfortable job and jump into a completely new line of consulting work. Within three weeks of making the leap, he found out that his wife was pregnant with their first child. All of a sudden there was much more riding on his decisions. Some people lamented his unfortunate timing. My friend says that, in hindsight, the timing couldn't have been better. Had he been worried about feeding his family, he might not have made the jump. The additional mouth to feed lit a fire in him that hadn't been quite there before, and the anxiety worked for him rather than against him. Because of his newfound motivation, he was willing to try absolutely everything, and to keep trying things until he found something that worked. He had no commitment to his approach, only to the guiding strategy of building this new business, serving his new clients, and reaching his goals.

You've crafted your unreasonable strategy, one that is going to break your business wide open. Next, you should spend a little time thinking about your thought process so that you can be prepared to make decisions on the road ahead.

CHAPTER 4

UNREASONABLE
THINKING

To arrive at the simplest truth, as Newton knew and practiced, requires years of contemplation. Not activity. Not reasoning. Not calculating. Not busy behavior of any kind. Not reading. Not talking. Not making an effort. Simply bearing in mind what it is one needs to know. And yet those with the courage to tread this path to real discovery are not only offered practically no guidance on how to do so, they are actively discouraged and have to set about it in secret, pretending meanwhile to be diligently engaged in the frantic diversions and to conform with the deadening personal opinions which are continually being thrust upon them.

—George Spencer-Brown, *The Laws of Form*

In being unreasonable, you seek to become aware of those boundaries that confine normal, acceptable behavior, and then deliberately step beyond them. This is not about getting outside the box. The unreasonable businessperson doesn't consider the existence of the box in the first place. It is not about breaking the rules. It is about abandoning the concept of rules altogether. It is not about codifying anything that could quickly outlive its usefulness. It is about finding more productive, more effective, and more flexible forms of behavior—ones that promote your immediate agenda; while they could have lasting value, they are just as likely to be good for this moment alone. To wrap your mind around these new ways of being requires having new thoughts. Creating new ideas, perhaps from bits and pieces of old ones, perhaps in ways more like pulling them from Carl Jung's collective unconscious or Ernest Holmes's Universal Mind, perhaps making them up new out of whole cloth.

Rules for Breaking the Rules

The biggest constriction on thinking is the existence of rules, so the first thing that unreasonable people in organizations must do is develop a healthy understanding of what rules are and what it means to break them. That way, when the time comes to break these rules, they aren't afraid.

Being unreasonable does not mean you should ignore the past and everything that has gone before. Rather it means accepting that your old rules were developed over time for a good reason. For the most part, these rules have worked and resulted in something valuable, but for whatever reason, they are no longer working. Here's the problem: you've grown to know and love the rules, and even if you hate them, you are comfortable operating within them. The very human drive to accept rules is deeply embedded, honed through millions of years of evolutionary pack behavior. Accepting rules has a strong survival value for our species, and violating this principle meets with distaste. Breaking rules is, at a very deep level, contrary to our nature. Thus, to break rules requires rules for rule breaking.

Rules about Breaking Rules

Anybody can break the rules. Rule breaking does not require any special status or title, like "manager" or "leader." The lowliest person on a team can become an effective rule breaker if she is given just a bit of leeway, as long as she does not believe that she will be punished too harshly as a result.

Rules are good only when they produce results that support a company's aims and goals. Otherwise, they're bad rules. This is the only true evaluation of a rule: does following the rule bring a company closer to realizing its aims and goals? If it doesn't, it is a bad rule and should be abandoned.

Good rules are in place to keep order, structure, and process and to maintain predictability. Bad rules are there to make someone's life easier in some way. Rules can (and do) easily change from good to bad over time. It helps to know why a rule was put in place so that you can understand the unintended consequences of breaking it. But no matter what, you absolutely must know why you are breaking it.

Both Good Rules and Bad Rules Can Be Broken

There are no rules that fit all situations. (Check the Ten Commandments if you don't believe this.) Our businesses and our lives are too complex for any simple guidelines to be 100 percent appropriate in all cases. This is not meant as an inducement to break very basic rules, such as core values. It means that when your beloved rule comes smack up against the fact that it's holding back progress, you should at least be willing to question whether the rule is still appropriate or whether it's some kind of holdover.

You will not be struck down if you break the rules. (You may be fired, however.) This means that it's worthwhile to weigh the risk of breaking any particular rule against the payoff of doing so. On the other hand, don't worry about "getting into trouble" if you're sure that your rule breaking will help deliver the goods. (See the discussion of permission later in this chapter.)

You don't have to be "the best" to make up your own rules, although it does help if you are. A certain amount of experience and insight is attributed to those who are the best, and if you are considered the best—at the top of the heap—it gives you a great deal of credibility and insulates you from a lot of backlash. On the other hand, making up your own rules may enable you to be the best.

Rule breakers are not lawbreakers. (Not necessarily, anyway.) Know the difference. If you find that breaking the rules will in fact break the law, and you still plan to break the rules, make sure that you are going to do so for a very good reason. Almost all of the time—unless you are deliberately setting an example or fighting for social change—it would be better to find another way of getting done whatever you are trying to do.

Break rules when your new approach will make you more effective, or when the old rules are simply not effective at all. Otherwise, why are you breaking the rules?

Leaders are typically more comfortable with breaking rules than the people below them are. In fact, that's a big chunk of what makes them leaders. Encourage your team to question rules that aren't supporting your organization's goals. By itself, this will help turn them into leaders.

Knowledge doesn't make something right. There's an old saw that if you don't know that there is a rule, you don't know enough to break it. This is nonsense and has nothing to do with rule breaking. Understand the situation you are in. Figure out why things aren't working and base your next actions on what will work. Of course, it helps to understand the prevailing environment, and you may try to avoid wanton rule breaking just for its own sake. Also, stepping on too many toes may be a bad idea in your company, and you may want to see if there are other, less contentious ways to go about achieving your goal. But in the end, if there's a rule in place and you inadvertently break it, see the next rule.

"It is easier to apologize than to get permission." Admiral Grace Hopper, the inventor of the COBOL computer programming language, said this. This august woman broke so many rules that it would make your head spin. If you ask for permission first, are told no, and do it anyway, you're really in trouble. So if you want to get anything important done, make sure not to ask. If you're certain that you're right, go ahead and do it. You'll probably find out more about the penalties later.

The rules for who should and should not break the rules are as follows: novices do not know the rules; amateurs know the rules, but have trouble following them; pros know the rules and can begin to bend them as necessary; and geniuses, who know the rules, break them, create new rules, and break those as well. Each of these people can break the rules as necessary. Even novices are allowed to break the rules, as they may have radically effective propositions based on their innocence.

—Anonymous

Creativity does not have to result in rule breaking. There are all sorts of ways to improve your results inside of the current rules, especially when those rules "make sense" and are working well. But most of the time, creativity does result in rule stretching.

Just because you break the rules doesn't mean you're a genius or an innovator. Rule breaking may produce no valuable results whatsoever. On the other hand, breakthroughs never happen without rule breaking. It's part of the definition.

When to Break the Rules

The only useful rule on when to break rules is that you should break the rules only when breaking them is better than not breaking them, and even this rule is questionable. Rule breaking should be done only when it's appropriate to the situation, and never for its own sake. There is no right time, right circumstance, right need, right risk-reward profile, right way to do it, or right anything else. All other rules on rule breaking are useless. But there are a number of guidelines, processes, and procedures that will help you think in a way that can get you outside the rules.

Once you've understood the rules and rule breaking, you are freer to think without fear about the implications of your thinking. The rest of this chapter details several ideas, processes, and tools to help you generate unreasonable ideas that can move your business forward.

Maverick Journalist Breaks the Rules

In 1994, Randy Cassingham was a technical writer at the Jet Propulsion Laboratory in Pasadena, California. Perhaps as a holdover from his journalism training, he was in the habit of clipping quirky news stories, which he posted outside his cubicle. Soon he developed a following among JPL's scientists and engineers. People would actually detour around the office so that they could check out what was new at Randy's cube. The traffic gave him his breakthrough idea, which he shared with disbelieving, discouraging colleagues. He was going to quit his secure, full-time job and make his living by publishing these oddities on the Internet.

Talk about unreasonable. At the time, the Internet was considered to be a pristine, unexploited commons. There were all sorts of cultural rules and norms in place forbidding commerce: nobody was going to sell anything, and certainly no one would be making any money. But Cassingham, seeing the future, charged ahead and ignored those rules. Not only was he going to make money on the Internet, he was going to do it in the weirdest way possible—by giving his products away for free! (If you think this is common now, it is. But not in 1994!)

While there's no way to know for sure, Randy's free newsletter, *This Is True*, may have been the first viral marketing success. From the first, he included something unusual in the copyright, saying, "Feel free to forward this newsletter unaltered to your friends." Passing from e-mail address to e-mail address, the publication rocketed to more than 100,000 subscribers and provided a compelling platform for paid advertising—just one more rule broken by this maverick. *This Is True* is now read by people in 204 countries and provides its owners a very comfortable income—something that not many journalists or writers can say—all because of Cassingham's willingness to ignore conventional wisdom.

Why and Why Not?

Simple is as simple does.

—Forrest Gump

A great many people think they are thinking, when they are merely rearranging their prejudices.

—William James, nineteenth-century psychologist and philosopher

Why and why not? These two brief questions hold the key to breaking rules that were once relevant, but no longer are. The tendency toward rule following hates these questions, because there are often no answers. Here's the point: if you can't get a straight explanation answering why or why not, then why should you follow the rule? If you do get an answer, listen carefully—one of three things can happen.

1. You can accept the answer as sane and valid, and move on with following the rule.
2. You can decide that the answer may once have made sense but that it is no longer valid. You decide that this rule is breakable, and you use the answer as a jumping-off point to formulate a new course of action. (Whether your new course of action becomes a rule or not is not the subject of this section!)
3. You can decide that the answer makes no sense at all. You probe further, but you get nowhere. You then choose to follow your conscience and do whatever you think makes sense.

This is what children do when they are trying to understand the world around them. They haven't been conditioned yet to just accept things. Whenever they hear a new rule (it sounds to them more like a command), they ask why. Whenever they're told not to do something, they ask why not. Grown-ups, however, have gotten so used to being told what to do that for the most part they don't question much of anything. After years in business, adults have developed the ingrained and unquestioned belief that someone has previously considered the issues and thought things through, and that the rule they are being told to follow has been tested, validated, checked for mistakes, optimized, and improved over time.

Right? Maybe not, but no matter, because most of us have chosen to accept that the rules we're following make sense. And even when things clearly don't make sense, most people have decided ahead of time to simply follow the rules.

Author Zig Ziglar tells his version of an old story:

This old boy down home, his wife sent him to the store for a ham. Upon bringing it home she asks him why he didn't have the butcher cut the ends off. Of course, he asks his wife why she wanted the ends cut off. She tells him that her mama has always done it that way and that was reason enough for her. "Well let's just find out more, okay?" he says. Since the wife's mama was visiting, his wife goes in to Mama and says, "Mama, why do you always cut the ends off the ham?" Mama replied that this was the way her mama did it; mother, daughter and "this old boy" then decide to call Grandma and solve this three-generation mystery. Grandma promptly replied that she cut the ends of the ham because her roaster was too small to cook the ham in one piece.

Questioning everything slows the pace down a bit, and it's a good way to irritate the people you're working with. When things are going as well as expected, there's no need for it. It's only when they're not going so well that you have to ask what's behind the rules. That's when you start to dig into the rationale; it may make sense and it may not. Sometimes you have to burrow down several layers to get anywhere—and only then do you find out that the whole process was based on a misinterpretation.

Make no mistake about it: asking a whole lot of why and why not questions will definitely make you appear unreasonable, even downright uncooperative, whether you're trying to be or not. People who put forth rules believe in them and do not want them questioned. At best, they'll see your behavior as tedious; at worst, they'll see it as troublemaking and disruptive. Don't let that stop you. Many deeply embedded rules do not make sense, but you do have to pick your spots.

Remember that being unreasonable is both a call to action and a frame of mind.

Author's Note: Really unreasonable people ask these questions no matter what because they are always trying to push the envelope. You may enjoy this route; just beware of the consequences. I do this all the time.

Breaking Compromises

I often wish that I could rid the world of the tyranny of facts. What are facts but compromises? A fact merely marks the point where we have agreed to let investigation cease.

—William Bliss Carman, Canadian poet

Most products, and, indeed, most companies, are built on compromises. For instance, if you sell a product at the lowest price, consumers in your market assume that your product is not of the highest quality. All people know that if they want higher quality, they'll have to pay for it, and lower prices mean that quality is down. *What would happen if you didn't have to make that trade-off?* How might you sell the best product on the market at a rock-bottom price? Asking this kind of question is critical, as the right answer could have huge implications for your company.

The ability to break compromises—and the unreasonable ideas that result from doing so—is a source of great breakthroughs. Compromises are concessions that you make in one aspect of your business so that you can further another aspect. This sounds benign, and because we're so used to it, it seems natural, as if it were some kind of definition of the way the world really is. Reasonable people know that you can't have everything, so you must decide which things you want most, and you compromise to get them. It's not only that high prices mean high quality; there's a whole service-quality-price triangle. You want to lower prices and keep quality high, and to do this, you reduce or eliminate service. That appears to make sense, but what if you discovered a new low-cost way to manufacture your product? What if you passed that reduced cost of goods on to your customers and kept your service approach level? Lower prices, same quality, same service.

You know you're listening to a compromise when someone says, "That's the way it's always been." "Always been" thinking makes it hard to see that compromises are not written in stone. Take this typical compromise: "We can't get enough talented people unless we pay higher salaries"—which leads to, "We can't afford to pay that much, so we can't grow quickly." This compromise is rooted in the idea that your business requires people with a certain level of skill, who are hard to find and therefore expensive, and you can't afford them. What if you lowered the level of skill required? How would you do that? By systemizing the production process in such a way that a less-experienced person could operate it just as well. What if on top of that you offered nonfinancial incentives or a training program designed to attract less experienced but equally talented staff.

In the United States, *capitated* health-care payments lead to long waits for doctor's appointments, which in turn lead to misuse of hospital emergency rooms. Unintended results include the following compromises: delayed diagnosis of chronic health problems and no posttreatment follow-up care, which together lead to higher costs for more complicated treatments in later disease stages and an overall lowering of care quality. *Urgent-care* facilities that utilize standard medical practices rather than emergency room medicine have been developed to break the compromise.

Compromises are usually the result of long-established presuppositions about the relationships between various aspects of your business, such as the supposed relationship between cost and quality. The key to breaking compromises is to reveal those presuppositions and break the linkages between unnecessarily related concepts.

Presuppositions are nothing more than beliefs—ideas that we think of as permanent and true. Most of the time these beliefs are so ingrained that they've become transparent; you can't even tell that they're there. In the price-quality-service triangle, we've cemented the linkage among these three. Why? Who knows, but every management book published prior to 1995 stresses this relationship, so it must be true. If we believe that the relationships are fixed, the laws of geometry mean that we can't make more than any two better at one time without worsening the third. The real meaning of the New Economy that sprang from the 1990s Internet revolution was that these three elements did not need to move in lockstep. By exposing the belief as a belief rather than an as objective set of facts we become willing to consider each element independently. Then—and only then—do we have the possibility of holding two of them steady while improving the third, enabling us to develop superior solutions.

When people think about staffing, they see a frozen relationship between the production process and its required skill level. We think that the process is complicated to operate and that people need experience in order to operate it. Actually, it's complicated only because no one's taken the trouble to simplify it. It requires experience because no one's documented it sufficiently. Once you uncouple the process from the people needed to run it, you can address ways to alter the staffing requirements. In the medical example, the relationship is one of exclusion. Because of the way insurers pay for services, doctors' offices have evolved to do one thing, and emergency rooms, because they are paid under a separate model, to do another. But what if you uncoupled the payment system from the service and eliminated the this-or-that relationship? You could create a new model, an *extension* of the doctor's office, which gives rise to the urgent-care facility.

To break compromises, you first have to be able to see that there is a compromise. Next, you must identify the various elements that are compromised and the linkages that bind those elements together. Then identify the presuppositions that drive the relationship to behave the way it does. Sometimes the compromise is so transparent that there's no way to see it. In these cases, you may be able to shed some light on it by conducting a *critical factors analysis*. Asking, "Why does this have to be this way?" or "What makes this behave this way?" or "What is the relationship between these things?" will reveal the presupposed relationships among the various elements.

If you ask, "Why do people go to hospital emergency rooms?" you'll find three main answers. There are people who go because their regular doctors are unavailable, say during the evening or on the weekend. There are people who go because they can't get an appointment in a doctor's office on short enough notice. And there are people who go because they know they'll be taken care of even if they can't pay. These last two are clearly not part of the original design, and now you know you're on to something. (There is, of course, a fourth answer—a genuine emergency requiring hospital-level care. Interestingly, that is not the primary reason people go!)

Once you've clarified the elements, the linkages between them, and the presuppositions that define those linkages, you can disengage one from the other. Start by breaking the compromise in your mind by knowing the relationship that you have to change. Find a way to alter one of the elements or conditions without affecting the others. It still may not be easy, but now you have a plan of action, and you've isolated the things about which to think.

Everyone knows that companies go through what Geoffrey Moore labeled the "technology adoption life cycle," in which the prices for products fall when they reach the mass distribution phase. Much of this is caused by the fact that the original outsized profits in a limited-supply market attract cost-cutting competitors, resulting in lowered margins. That's OK, because the distribution volumes of the mass market also lower manufacturing costs, so although margins shrink, there are still enough profits to go around. All managers understand this and expect to make the compromise (higher volume times reduced margins), because when they do the math, the smaller margins on higher volumes still work out positively for the shareholders. Everyone knows this—except Steve Jobs that is. He and his team at Apple Computer figured out that the reverse could also be true. Apple used massive marketing and promotion to transform the financial results from mass distribution of the iPod. Instead of lowering the consumer price, the company used monster brand awareness and "hipness factor" to create an unbeatable luxury fashion accessory. The iPod has successfully resisted price erosion from numerous cheaper competitors and has launched a dynasty of iPod versions, every one priced higher than comparable offerings. Profits from the iPod have been staggeringly high and have lifted Apple from the brink of corporate death to one of the most profitable and highly valued consumer technology companies in the world.

As of this writing, Apple's earnings growth is 50 percent higher than that of any competitor or comparable company—and this is 100 percent due to the iPod.

Breaking important compromises will always end up creating breakthroughs in your business.

The Opposite of Truth

The opposite of a correct statement is a false statement. But the opposite of a profound truth may well be another profound truth.

—Niels Bohr, physicist

When you are getting what you want by being reasonable, you don't have to think about being *un*reasonable. When you aren't getting it, you have to step outside of your existing thought models and develop a new approach. One simple way to do that is to take the things you are currently doing, thinking, and believing, and reverse them. Now you can use that reversed idea as a jumping-off point for further thinking.

Suppose you are seeking more customers. (Who isn't?) Reverse that thought and what do you get? You're looking for fewer customers. If that were true, what would it mean for your business? Since you'd have fewer customers, those you did have would need to spend far more money. What would those customers be like? (*Hint:* They'd probably have more money than your current ones.) Where would you find such customers? How would you reach them? What would you say to them? How would you have to change your business to please them? What could you offer them to induce them to spend more? When you answer those questions, you may stumble upon a breakthrough.

Perhaps you run a consulting firm, and your big problem is that you are expanding the business and your marketing team is bringing in clients by the bushel. But you don't believe you'll be able to service these clients because you're having trouble attracting the right level of talented professionals, each of whom can handle only a limited number of clients. Reverse that "truth." What if each of my staff members were responsible for a limited number of clients? Perhaps you'll start to wonder about how to service more clients with the same personnel. What aspects of your consulting solution could be automated? What elements of your service offering could be systemized? What if you created forums and group mastermind programs? There are all sorts of solutions to this question, and they'd be right in front of you if only you'd ask the right questions.

Here are some typical truths and the questions that arise when you reverse them.

The Truth	Questions That Come from Reversing This Truth
We need more customers.	How can we make more money by having fewer customers?
We need more staff to expand our business.	How can we serve more clients with the same staff, or even with fewer staff?
We don't have enough time to get everything done. We're going to have to work harder.	How can we do more in less time while working less?
We need to expand our Web presence.	How can we stand out from the crowd by using offline marketing?
Our competitors are forcing us to lower prices.	How can we gain even more business by raising our prices?
The customer is always right.	The customer is often wrong; how can we turn that into a growth opportunity?
We have to lower prices to get greater market share.	How can we use our high price position to attract better clients?
Support revenues should be 50 percent of the total revenue.	How can we make more money by outsourcing all our support or, better yet, building an offering that never requires support?

Our customers want greater selection.	How can we profit by having a limited selection of exclusive products?
Our clients want more service.	How can we offer less service and turn that into a selling point?
Support costs are driving us crazy.	How can we turn support into a profit center?
We have to outsource our support offshore. It's the only way we can afford it.	How can we insource and create our own low-cost support company?
It takes too long to build a brand.	How can we use our brand-X status to build faster name recognition?

Every single aspect of the rental car business is one giant compromise for the consumer, as if it were all designed to be as easy as possible for the rental companies—and that's close to the truth. Car rental offices are often located on cheap real estate, which means that it is inconvenient to pick up your car and just as inconvenient to return it. Except at airports and in the largest cities, rental offices are not open late. Offices often have long waiting lines because of tons of redundant paperwork, including endless signatures and copious fine print, all of which must be initialed. Customers must pay on a 24-hour basis, even though that rarely matches their car needs. There are numerous hard-to-understand options, along with mandatory "surcharges." And, since fuel is not included, you have to fill the tank when you return the car, and if you don't, you don't even want to think about the price of the gas. Everyone who's ever rented a car knows these things—they are the sad but accepted truths of renting a car.

How many of those truths can you reverse at once? What if you created a system that reversed (and vanquished) all of them? Zipcar, a Web-based car rental company that bills itself as a "self-service car sharing company," was founded to do just that. The company's vision? *"Providing reliable and convenient access to on-demand transportation, complementing other means of mobility."*

Does that sound like a car rental company? Zipcar implemented every New Economy idea in the book and made extensive use of technology, including the Internet, wireless networking, the Global Positioning System (GPS), and radio-frequency-ID (RFP) technology. The entire business is self-service, with all reservations being made via a Web interface, which means no waiting on long lines. There are no offices to get to; cars are left in convenient locations around town. And since there are no offices, there are no office hours—the company operates 24 hours a day. Rentals can be by the hour or the day or the week, so you use the car as much or as little as necessary. And everything—local taxes, insurance, fuel, even satellite radio—is included in the price. The company's financial numbers are private, but press releases indicate that the company is growing much faster than 100 percent each year.

Think Bigger

In his 1959 classic *The Magic of Thinking Big*, David J. Schwartz tells us that thought governs action, actions govern results, and the size of our thoughts affects and multiplies the size of those results. According to Schwartz, thinking small and producing limited results is no easier than thinking big, expending an equal amount of effort, and producing huge results. Those who earn five times your income aren't likely to be five times smarter, better, or luckier—they are simply thinking five times bigger. But he also says that you have to want it, and that one's desire may be the best kept secret ingredient for success.

While there are many differences between Bill Gates and someone who starts a software consultancy to support his family, the main difference is that Gates had a vision of changing the world by putting a personal computer on every office desktop and in every home. Now that's thinking big! Henry Ford outstripped his competitors with a vision of putting a car in every American garage.

Reasonable people scale their aspirations to what they feel they can wrap their arms around or wrap their brains around. But perhaps in a more limiting way they also scale to what they think other people will perceive as normal. Reasonable people don't want to be scorned for having grandiose visions and being full of themselves. Many people are told by their parents and teachers not to get "ahead of themselves" and to take it one step at a time. So thinking small is considered reasonable, whereas thinking big is not. Thinking big is definitely unreasonable. It is beyond all the preconceptions most people have about themselves and their abilities. And it is a fast way to create big results. Indeed, it may be a requirement for creating big results.

Gates and Ford are two well-known examples. Small business coach Michael Port is another. "It's unreasonable to think that people want to think bigger about what they offer the world. Who knows, but the only way I find out is if I put something out in the world and see what people do in response. I played it small as an actor; I played it safe. Perhaps that's why I failed. Now, I make everything public and can't play it safe anymore."

Big and public, that's what makes Port successful. He does everything in full view. If he has an idea, he creates a Web site and invites people to participate. Then he harnesses their collaborative energy to improve it, promote it, and make it bigger until it takes on a life of its own. This model is very different from the more reasonable way most companies proceed. They try to control their ideas; they build them in secret and let the products out only when they're "ready." What's so surprising is that Port says that he has a thin skin and is quite concerned that people like him, so he finds all this visibility a bit scary. That may be what makes him so unreasonable—he does it anyway. Port really believes this stuff; one of his projects is called the Think Big Revolution, which is an online community of people supporting one another as they work to "stand for something" and, well, "think big." In fact, he guarantees that participants will think bigger about who they are and what they offer the world.

Rather than sell people things, I invite them to my environment and ask
them if they want to do cool things with me. I invite them and so far
they're coming. I believe in the power of all the people in my environment
rather than in my own specialness. Lots of people talk about this.
You have to be able to actually do it.

—Michael Port

Thinking from the Future

Paul Scheele, the wizard behind the widely used accelerated learning system PhotoReading, says that normal people spend 20 percent of the time identifying a solution and then 80 percent of the time making it work. Unreasonable people switch this around and spend 80 percent of the time on defining the problem and coming up with a solution. Then the 20 percent of time that is spent on the mechanics is much more effective. Conventional Western-style medicine is so popular because it quickly offers a solution to get rid of symptoms. But the symptoms often return, just in a different form. This happens because we jump to solutions too quickly and don't deal with the root cause. So we solve the apparent problem, which leads to some unintended result. Then we solve *that* problem, which leads to another unintended result, and so on. Scheele calls this an oscillation (problem/solution/problem/solution/problem . . .). One of the reasons we get oscillations is that reasonable people search for solutions in the *historical past*; in other words, they find something that worked before and use it again. But since the solution is a historical one, it is often maladapted to the current problem, resulting in the unintended result.

What if you take the mindset that a *creative* solution will—by definition—look quite different from what you expected? Some creative people go so far as to consider that the desired solution may look like something that they didn't want at all. Thinking unreasonably requires transcending the historical mind, the preconceived mind, and instead using what Scheele calls "the primordial mind." Think of *primordial* as being similar to *virgin* or *fresh*.

Consider this: analysts at the Mental Research Institute did a little experiment where they asked people to rate themselves on various criteria, using a scale of 1 to 10. No matter what rating the subject gave, if the experimenter then followed with, "Why did you say that and not higher?" subjects would explain by stating everything that was wrong with them. If the experimenter asked, "Why did you say that and not lower?" subjects would talk about all their good personal qualities. In other words, their responses were more dependent on programming embedded in the interviewer's question than in some understanding of their pasts.

You can control your thinking by asking yourself the right questions. If you want to have unreasonable thoughts, ask unreasonable questions that require unreasonable answers. It's as easy as that.

In 1985, Scheele was hired by IDS/American Express to apply accelerated learning techniques on a project to help people absorb information more quickly. When his company, Learning Strategies, focused its thinking on reading, most of what it came up with was a lot like reading, only faster. IDS was after something more powerful. When Scheele asked the question differently, eliminating reading as part of the problem formulation, he came up with a completely new model. He simply asked how we can "input" this information directly into the brain in a way that will let us retrieve it later. That didn't sound like reading anymore, and the company hit on the concept of "mental photography," enabling the other-than-conscious part of the mind to record images of the printed page at superhigh speeds. The result was Scheele's internationally successful Photo Reading program.

Be Afraid of the Right Thing

> *Only the unknown frightens men. But once a man has faced the unknown, that terror becomes the known.*
>
> —Antoine de Saint-Exupéry

All unreasonable things—because they challenge the conventional norms, the tried and true, the accepted wisdom—have an element of danger attached to them. And with danger comes fear. Being unreasonable—being willing to challenge the status quo and deviate from the norm—has nothing to do with being fearless. It is more like being courageous. Courage is neither the absence of fear nor the willingness to do dangerous things. Courage is acting in the face of fear.

In the middle of the pack, life is steady and safe, and that's why people tend to prefer it. But out on the edge of things, the world is more complicated, dangerous, and filled with risk. Deal with it. Thankfully, by virtue of evolution, we are prepared to do just that. There is a little piece of genetic wiring in the brain that seems to be designed to take note of changes in the environment; scientists call it the reticular activating system, or RAS. It is a part of the primitive brain stem. Like many parts of the brain, its function is obscure, but it seems to be involved with evaluating whether things that are happening in the world are benign or dangerous. Although it probably evolved to help us take note of saber-toothed tigers or shifts in the weather, the RAS seems to facilitate detection of a wide range of opportunities and threats.

This means that when something threatening approaches, our senses sharpen, and we can see it coming, increasing our odds of survival. The knowledge that you have this built-in early warning system should mitigate your fear. This could be important, since being unreasonable means that your agitation level is always going to be a bit higher than normal. If you're not scared of anything, it's a sure sign that you are playing a safe game and not doing anything worth doing.

All significant ventures push the envelope. Being on the cutting edge is part of what makes them meaningful in the first place, and by their very nature, breakthrough ventures are fraught with uncertainty and risk. The wrong move, bad timing, or just plain rotten luck can threaten your finances, your reputation, your career, your health, and possibly your longevity. Unreasonable people are often afraid, and rightly so. So what? Just be sure you are afraid of the right thing. Unfortunately, we often focus our fears on the wrong thing.

Jorge was a surgeon who had come to the point in life where he hated his medical practice. The way he tells it, becoming a doctor was a foregone conclusion from the day he was born: his father was a doctor, his two older brothers were doctors, his sister was a doctor. Being the youngest member of his family, he felt that he had no choice but to follow in their footsteps. Eleven years into his practice, he finally admitted how much he disliked his life. Each day was more difficult and painful than the last. Two big issues held him in place, his standing within his family and his doctor's salary. Notwithstanding these powerful influences, he finally reached a point where he was unwilling to spend any more time doing surgery and boldly left active practice to become a patients' rights advocate and author.

Two years later, although he was emotionally fulfilled by his new career, the money still wasn't coming in. His wife was pressuring him to return to surgery, and he was giving it serious consideration. He had been offered a job as a staff surgeon, and he was going to take it. He called me for advice. Jorge told me that he was afraid—afraid that he would never be able to support his family. I probed for details about the position, and I uncovered what going back to surgery would mean to him. I told him that, indeed, he was right to be afraid, but he was fearful of the wrong thing. He needed to be afraid of giving up on his new life. He needed to be afraid of turning back to the life he so deeply hated. He needed to be afraid of quitting on his dream.

Courage is not fearlessness. Being fearless is often senseless. Fear, like pain, is tremendously useful; that's why we have an RAS in the first place. We want to be alert to potential dangers, and fear—properly channeled—primes us for action. It's fear that has us take off and run faster when that saber-toothed tiger jumps out from the brush. Fear is a powerful ally.

But be afraid of the right things. Fears that work in your favor are fears that keep you from being complacent. They keep you focused on the threats you can do something about and on the situations you can take advantage of. In Jorge's case, he was afraid of not being able to support his family. He was also afraid of his wife's leaving him unless he earned some money. By redirecting his fears of taking a life-depressing job, he strengthened his motivation to succeed financially in his otherwise fulfilling new career. His fear of regressing to his old life gave him the kick in the pants he needed to market and sell himself effectively.

You have to face your fears. That's what courage is about. You've chosen to be unreasonable so that you can accomplish great things. Fear is part of the package. Don't let it stop you.

But what if you're afraid of the wrong things? The wrong fears are the ones that cause you to pull back from your vision. These are the fears that cause you to freeze in your tracks and stop acting. It's easy to tell the difference. Fears that cause you to take action are generally good; fears that cause you to seize up are generally bad. The thing to do with the "bad" fears, the ones that make you less effective, is to figure out what's really causing them.

In Jorge's case, he was afraid that his chosen career was never going to allow him to take care of his family. Some digging revealed that what was behind this fear was pretty basic: not knowing how to make his new business profitable. Instead of worrying about making a transition yet again, he was able to redirect his attention to the issue of business development. His original fear was not irrational; it just wasn't going to help him get what he wanted.

One typical fear that business owners deal with regularly is that of competitors sneaking up on them. This fear can be interpreted in a few ways. If the owners are worried about going out of business, that's a bad fear that can paralyze them. If instead, this fear causes them to worry about how to improve the company's positioning and how to generate more leads, driving them toward more effective marketing, that fear can be energizing.

Andy Grove, the former CEO of Intel, is famous for saying, "When it comes to business, I believe in the value of paranoia." Grove wasn't kidding about his paranoia; he was simply afraid of the right things.

Because it will drive you toward the unknown and uncharted, being unreasonable will increase your general level of anxiety. Make sure that when this happens, you fear the right things, not things that your mother or some previous boss taught you. Use fear as a friend. Get focused on the most important problems. Dig down to understand what is behind your discomfort and develop new solutions. Use fear to generate breakthroughs.

What should you be afraid of? Here's a short list of things that could rightfully give you pause—and perhaps a few sleepless nights:

Arrogance
Ignorance
Complacency
Competitors sneaking up on you
(You should also fear an obviously false belief that you are
    untouchable and unbeatable.)
Disruptive technologies
Unreasonable business models (other people's, that is)
Globalization
(If you're not part of the solution, you are part of
    the problem.)
Not having enough capital
Overly optimistic sales forecasts
Unsustainable business designs
Loss of focus
False beliefs you are sure are real
Statistics
Yes-men and yes-women
Reasonableness

Of course, there are dozens of other ideas, states of mind, market situations, and financial conditions that are healthy targets of fear. But do make sure that you can do something about the situations you dwell on. That's what makes them healthy and productive.

Give Up Your Prejudices

*Everyone is a prisoner of his own experience. No one can eliminate
prejudices—just recognize them.*

—Edward R. Murrow

The Nobel Prize–winning physicist Paul Dirac said, "Great
breakthroughs in physics always involve giving up some great
prejudice." What's true of physics is true of business as well. Your
prejudices—adverse judgments or opinions formed beforehand
or without knowledge or examination of the facts—evolved from
your past experiences. You may think of your prejudices, when
you are aware of them at all, as being handy shortcuts to avoid
having to figure it all out again. That's a nice spin on things; it
makes you seem very efficient and such, yet prejudices are always
bad. They will keep you from seeing the reality of your situation,
since you already "know" the way things are. Great opportunities in business always come from changes that are happening
now; if you remain blinded by prejudices, you won't see the
changes until it's too late.

Prejudices are knee-jerk brain functions that we substitute for
thinking, so the first step in letting go of them is to become consciously aware of them. Prejudices typically evolve from some
strong learning that occurred in response to a similar situation
in a completely different context. Generally, the situation had
some high emotional content associated with it—either you
won big or you lost big, causing the prejudice to get locked into
your brain.

Consciousness occurs when an organism becomes aware of its
own existence. Your job is to become (and remain) aware of what's
going on in your own brain. Recognize when you are repeating
the same thoughts over and over in response to similar circumstances. This is a sure sign that you aren't really thinking, but are
merely replaying some old tapes that no longer fit. (Old tapes
never do.) Another way to catch yourself in the act is by questioning whether the thoughts in your head make any sense in the

current context. If they don't, that is one more sign that those thoughts are holdovers from some past experience.

When you set out to do some thinking about a particular subject, it is useful to examine what you already think. Start by making a list of the beliefs you hold about the issue at hand. List them, and then, one by one, write down why you think each of these beliefs is actually true. Take this one step further and write down—if you can remember—where each belief originally came from. Now that you know what's been going on inside your head, you have a chance to evaluate it. Ask the following questions: Is this idea still true? Does this belief make it easier to solve this issue, or harder? Should I still believe this?

It can be difficult to let go of ingrained prejudices, mostly because you can't see them for what they are. This process will help loosen the hold that an idea has on you. Once you start to question old, out-of-date beliefs, they will weaken. Keep it up and they'll eventually fall away.

Do this same process with your team. First ask people to do this on their own, then get everyone together and put all the beliefs on a whiteboard so that you can tear them apart one by one. This exercise has the potential to blow your entire project wide open.

Create a Brain Trust

Only a fool thinks that he alone has all the answers.

—Chinese proverb

Once you've decided that you are stepping beyond your beliefs and boundaries, you'd better get some help. Because you may be a prisoner of your own mindset (who isn't?), thinking by yourself may not get you very far. A sure way to deal with this is to create a brain trust to help you think things through.

What's a brain trust? Also called a mastermind, a brain trust is a group of smart, thinking people who will help you hammer out your ideas. Having a brain trust is like having your own private think tank to which you can turn to get answers, challenge your ideas, and get the benefit of other people's experience.

The brain trust, or mastermind alliance, was invented by Napoleon Hill, the author of *Think and Grow Rich*, who based his book on hundreds of interviews with industrial legends such as Henry Ford, Thomas Edison, and Edison's sponsor, Andrew Carnegie. Hill discovered that Ford, Edison, and tire magnate Harvey Firestone had a brain trust alliance and met regularly to brainstorm all their business interests. The brain trust, they said, multiplied their ability to think creatively and come up with unique and powerful solutions to their business issues. Today this principle is used in many companies—Disney, for instance, brings together teams of "Imagineers" (Disney staff members) to brainstorm and create new opportunities.

Implement this principle for your business by gathering teams of your best minds for the express purpose of multiplying your ability to think. Your brain trust may be made up of great minds from inside your business or from outside, and you may have more than one of these mastermind groups going at one time. It may include people who are intimate with your industry or those who know nothing about it. Choose people who will contribute and are not shy about sharing their thoughts. Also, choose people who are not afraid to hurt your feelings and will call plays as they see them. Expose your issues and your ideas to your brain trust and ask the members for their very best.

You can call your brain trust together for regular meetings or only when there is a particular problem to crack. Other people can see things through fresh eyes while you just keep seeing the same things over and over again. Their experiences are different; their contexts are different; their perspectives are different. How can their ideas not be different? Your brain trust can be especially useful for stepping out beyond the norms of your company and your industry, because the thinking these people bring to the table isn't grounded in either.

Take Fridays Off

Steady thinking is hard work, and people who are engaged in unreasonable business behavior are often working very hard indeed. That's because they are trying to accomplish something important, and that takes time. It is not unusual for people to work 40, 50, 60, maybe even 80 hours a week, which—over time—can create some pretty stale thinking. At some point, creative juices just stop flowing, and time at work will become counterproductive. As you keep putting in more and more time you become less and less effective, with the result that each task takes longer and longer. When that happens, *take Fridays off.*

Get out of the office and let your mind go. Do whatever it is you need to do to re-create yourself. Golf. Tennis. Lying by the pool. Hiking in the woods. Reading a novel in your library. Mowing the lawn. Taking a long drive. Riding your bike. Playing chess. Going to the movies. Anything that will get your mind off your work so that you can power down and recharge your creative batteries.

Taking time off to get more done is counterintuitive (good ideas often are) and may be frowned upon in your organization. No matter—call it a mental health day and consider taking a tax deduction for your day's expenses because they are work-related. Often, taking time off is necessary for being unreasonable. Weekend time doesn't count; that time is usually already spoken for. It's weekday time you need—playing hooky when you are supposed to be hard at work has its own restorative properties. Cutting your workweek by 8 or 10 hours won't lessen your workload, but it won't increase it, either—you'll simply have to be more effective the rest of the time at work.

Look to Other Industries

Each industry has its own biases and methods of doing business. What is commonplace in one industry may seem radical in another. A great method of stepping outside of the constrictions of your business and generating breakthroughs is to examine industries unrelated to yours and find ways to adopt their methods to your situation.

This works because as different as one business may be from another, there are a surprisingly small number of core strategies. Most of them are derived from military strategies and are based in armed conflict. The following list, taken from an anonymous ancient text, is quite comprehensive: you can attack your enemies from the front; attack from behind; attack their flank or encircle them; concentrate your forces or spread them thinly; become nimble and harry your enemies like a small dog; use misdirection and appear to be where you are not; use superior forces or superior weapons or superior speed; announce your presence or surprise them or hide in plain sight; attack them on the battlefield or lay waste their homeland; interdict their supply lines; attack their neighbors and allies; attack them politically; or lay siege to their fortresses.

Every one of these military strategies has an analogue in business, either in conflicts with your competitors or—to the distress of many—in your relationships with your clients and stakeholders. There are specific adaptations in manufacturing, supply, logistics, distribution, financing, sales, and marketing. The total list is not long, and its limited nature means that people in other industries have addressed the same problems you are now facing, although they've often dealt with them in different ways.

LifeWings, whose CEO Steve Harden was a U.S. Navy Top Gun instructor, teaches something called Crew Resource Management to surgical teams in hospitals. This unique method of structuring communication and systemizing procedures makes it much harder to make mistakes and ends up eliminating what the medical community terms "wrong surgeries." The sales process for persuading hospitals to use this wonderful tool is what is called a complex sale, which means that many people are involved in making the purchase decision, and the process can take a long time. Harden observed that unless the hospital's CEO or chief medical officer was involved, the likelihood of closing the sale was slim to none. But although the CEO or CMO was the ultimate decision maker, he or she usually was not part of the sales process itself. MDs are traditionally shielded from salespeople, preferring to be buffered by mediators like vice presidents, CFOs, and risk managers. Harden changed the rules of the game by taking a cue from the software industry's playbook, an industry that shares the problems LifeWings faced concerning access to decision makers. In fact, the typical scenario is almost identical, but in the software industry, they'd already figured out a solution. Simply, gently, but strongly tell your prospect: no access to the CEO, no sales presentation. This way, if the prospect thinks your solution is a good one, she has to grant you access. Talk about unreasonable! Imagine telling the prospect that you're unwilling to speak with her further unless she sets up a meeting.

"Be reasonable," they say. "We can't have that meeting. Dr. X simply won't fit it into his schedule." The norm is that doctors are able to stand apart, and all reasonable people respect that. Yet that's exactly what LifeWings didn't do. Instead, it took a stand and pressed the point. You can do this when your product is better than what the other guys have. "If you want our solution," Harden told prospects, "you have to set up the meeting. That's the only way we're going to be able to help you get what you want." The great news for everyone—the hospital, the patients, and LifeWings—was that it worked. Sales cycle time is down and sales are way up.

Seek ideas from other industries when the reasonable approaches in your industry aren't working as well as you'd like. How do you figure out what to do? Look for businesses that are structured similarly to yours in some way and that have problems similar to yours. Read their trade publications and newsletters, attend their conferences, even hire their consultants. Find out how they solve those problems. Are those processes adaptable to your situation? If so, try them on and make them fit.

PO-tential Thinking

Those who cannot remember the past are condemned to repeat it.

—George Santayana

When you're the first person whose beliefs are different from what everyone else believes, you're basically saying, "I'm right and everyone else is wrong." That's a very unpleasant position to be in. It's at once exhilarating and at the same time an invitation to be attacked.

—Larry Ellison, cofounder of Oracle

"PO!" says Edward de Bono.

PO?

Yes, PO, a word that de Bono says stands somewhere between yes and no but that has a meaning quite distinct from both. It's a word designed to generate movement, while suspending judgment about the value of that movement. PO stands for provocative operation, and de Bono suggests that many thorny problems can be solved by "destabilizing the mind," shaking it loose from its preconceptions, and driving it outside the rut of timeworn patterns. It's like annealing metal. Steel crystals form a lattice that, although stable, is not very strong. Heating it to a high enough temperature destabilizes the crystals' arrangement, causing them to re-form into another pattern that is much stronger.

PO destabilizes the crystal lattice of your mind, yielding possibly stronger ideas. How does it work? De Bono offers this example: there aren't enough licensed taxi drivers in the City of London. Instead of advancing a particular solution that is most likely based on previous conceptions, you advance a provocation, something that is designed not to offer a solution but to make people think about things differently from the way they have previously thought about them.

PO is used to begin a sentence, such as, "PO, the taxi driver does not know his way around." This does not imply that you support such an idea, just that the idea exists. Now people start to think. "Well, *what if* taxi drivers didn't know their way around? Then what? Well, then these cabs wouldn't be much good, except . . . except that they could be used only by residents, because residents can tell the driver the way to go. They could have a question mark on top of them. They could be cheaper. They could be used as "training cabs," where the drivers learn and get paid at the same time. Also, because they could be used only by residents, it would relieve the competition from tourists for cabs. All of these ideas flow from the PO provocation, and they actually start to make sense, crystallizing into a potentially powerful solution.

Or take this example. PO, planes land upside down. Stemming from this provocation is the idea of the negative lift that would come from having upside-down wings. From this idea comes the idea of adding negative lift to planes by using small upside-down wings. In an emergency, pilots need some extra lift *very quickly*, which is quite hard to engineer. By adding upside-down winglets to a plane, there would always be a bit of negative lift, which could be immediately canceled (by rotating the wings or using ailerons), giving pilots a ready source of much-needed positive lift.

PO provocations are not presupposed to be right or wrong; they simply exist, and they generate movement from which you can go forward toward new ideas. The PO formalism helps people avoid judging either the provocation or the responses; this lack of judgment—quite unreasonable for a group of people of any size—is well known to enhance the creative process. This method is so effective that during a recent workshop Dr. de Bono held at a steel factory in South Africa, 20 people generated 21,000 new ideas in an afternoon. PO provocations themselves are always unreasonable—breaking with the past, breaking with the norms—because they are always ideas that have never been tried, and perhaps have never even been heard of, like "cars have square wheels" or "robots raising children."

The purpose of this book is not to tell you how to think; that would be creating yet more rules to follow, which, of course, you'd eventually have to break. Instead, see these ideas as opportunities to think differently. Try them on, starting anywhere you like; each one will take you someplace different. Apply the rules for breaking rules, or PO-tential thinking. Maybe you need to break the compromises you've previously accepted, or perhaps you should take a look at other industries. Sometimes the lever you need to create a breakthrough idea is simply to take Friday off, get out of the office, and give your brain trust a call. It helps to let go of your prejudices. Unreasonable ideas are just a flight of fancy away.

Now that you've chosen an unreasonable strategy and opened up a new approach to thinking about your business, it's time to select the tactics that will help you reach your goals. These will not be marketing tactics or sales tactics, but unreasonable tactics. At least, some opening ones.

UNREASONABLE TACTICS

While a list of core business strategies is going to be limited, a similar list of business tactics is literally endless. Tactics are the specific maneuvers or procedures you will employ to actually accomplish something. For instance, your strategy may be to employ broadcast media and reach a broad, hard-to-identify audience; the specific tactic might be late-night direct-response television infomercials. This chapter is not going to be an encyclopedia of business tactics. Far from it. Instead of a catalog that would span several library shelves, this chapter contains a handful of unreasonable tactics that are meant to illustrate approaches that violate the norms most of us embrace. These tactics may fit your business and be immediately useful, or they may not. In either case, they are intended to give you a jumping-off point to energize your unreasonable thinking.

The Truth about Pricing

The first unreasonable tactic has to do with pricing. Cutting price is one of the oldest, most often used, most *reasonable* sales strategies in the book. It seems like plain old common sense. After all, everyone does it, but that doesn't mean that you should. When you cut your prices, you may make the sale, but your profits will sink like a rock in water. Winning dollars becomes worse than losing them. Take a look.

Suppose your product costs you $70 to manufacture, and you sell it for $100. For each sale, you earn $30, a profit margin of 30 percent. Now a tough customer walks in. He tells you that he was on the Internet and saw an overseas company that sells a product similar to yours for cheap. He haggles. He whines. You decide that a reduced price beats no sale, so you take $20 off and offer to sell the product for $80. Now, $80 might still seem like a good payday, until you do the math. The 20 bucks you lopped off didn't come from your costs (after all, you paid your jobbers full price for their materials and services). The 20 evaporated dollars came out of your gross profits, which pay for your time and everything else that your company provides.

You've just made your time and your company less valuable. Instead of earning a profit of 30 percent, you've reduced it to 13 percent. Your 20 percent price reduction has cost you 67 percent of your profits. You now earn less than one-half of what you were earning previously. Do you want to run a business where you make only one-half of what you should be making?

You might argue that $13 beats $0 hands down. But price reductions tend to have a downward spiral effect on a business. The lower price often becomes the new price, and stays low. In our example, that $100 product you just sold is, sorry to say, now an $80 product. Why? Other customers will find out about your price concession and demand the same for themselves.

What's worse is that word can spread to your competitors, making them feel as if they have to lower their own prices. Suddenly, you're in a price war, which will drop your profit margin even lower. Before you use price cutting as a sales tactic with people who are hesitating over money, try some other approach to close the deal. Here are four such approaches:

1. *Make trade-offs.* When prospects say, "I can't pay what you're asking," you say, "What part of my offer would you like me to remove so that we can drop the price?" In other

words, you'll take less money, but the value you're giving will be commensurately less.

2. *Stretch payment periods.* Sometimes prospects think that your price is fair but still can't afford it. If so, ask for half your money up front and half on the back end. Or if you feel strongly enough about your product, get the entire amount on the back end. Or, arrange lease payments that your prospects make for 24 months. Be creative.

3. *Offer extras.* Rather than lowering your price, throw in extras, such as free installation, an extended warranty, tickets to a workshop, or a printed manual. Ideally, the items you offer should cost you next to nothing, but they should have a high perceived value to your prospects.

4. *Make the beginning free.* Offer your prospects free initial periods of service if they sign long-term deals.

Here's an example of this last tactic. A software company client of mine had a customer who bought its big-ticket software, but who balked at paying the extra 18 percent the company wanted for an ongoing software maintenance agreement. Doesn't sound like a big problem, right? Wrong.

In the software business, a customer without a maintenance contract is likely to turn mean. Why? Since the customer knows it'll cost him every time he picks up the phone for technical support, he tries to wing it when he has a question or a problem. The result? The customer doesn't know how to use the product, doesn't get the right level of service, and doesn't get as much productivity out of the product as he had hoped. Even though it's his fault for skimping, he'll point the finger at you and bad-mouth your company.

What did the software company do? It offered the customer a four-year, noncancelable maintenance contract, with the first year for free. The customer signed. Why was this deal a success? Although the first-year-free strategy meant a 25 percent reduction in the total purchase price of the maintenance contract, the per-year price stayed the same. While the software company never lowered its publicized yearly fee, the customer got the break, and the company wasn't seen as a price cutter. The company benefited in other ways, too: the agreement locked up the customer for longer than the usual time period and gave the company opportunities to sell the customer additional products and services. Do the unreasonable: don't cut your prices. Figure out ways of keeping them high while giving customers excellent value.

As you can see, unreasonable pricing tactics can easily double your gross margin, and in many cases add a lot more than that. The next group of tactics revolves around how you make investment and budgeting decisions.

Are You Spending Enough?

To the untrained ear, or any ear abused by decades of loud music, most brands of audio speakers sound similar. But not Bose. Founded by Amar G. Bose, an MIT professor of electrical engineering, to create a speaker that sounded "natural," the company pioneered research in psychoacoustics (the study of how humans perceive sound), and its speakers were so distinct that Bose salespeople were able to sell their speaker systems door to door demonstrating their rich sound. Bose consistently ranks as the most trusted brand among top technology companies, and in 2006 it ranked second only to Sony in what marketers call "repurchase intent."

How does Bose do it? It's simple—the company spends a lot of money making its products great. While most companies apportion a limited percentage of revenues to research and development, Bose invests 100 percent of the company's profits in developing new products. Bose invested tens of million of dollars over 19 years in developing its headset technology. Now those headsets are a major part of the business; you see them on the heads of well-heeled flyers every time you step on an airplane. Bose speakers are also found in many high-end automobiles.

Speaking of the company's legendary research budget, President Bob Maresca says, "We are not in it strictly to make money." But, of course, all that investment generates a lot of cash indeed. Bose sales have risen more than 38 percent in the last year alone, and it controls 20 percent of the home audio market.

Common Sense Says Save Money

Bose's approach to research is unreasonable, and it is not the right solution for every company. But many companies look to control costs and find ways to reduce budget expenditures. Common sense says that you need to watch your expenses, and companies like Bose do just that, *but not in the important areas*.

It makes sense to control your spending in every area that cannot produce a return on your investment, and it is up to you to understand your company's expense structure well enough to know what will and will not produce a positive ROI. Will that fancy new office façade or super-luxury private jet bring in more, higher-paying clients? It may not. Will those high-end hotels padding the travel budget improve profits? What about your ego-building television campaign?

Think of it this way: there are three types of expenses in every company. First, there are those that are neither essential nor productive, such as nonperforming television advertising; these should be cut completely. Second, there are those that do not produce a return but that are essential to the company's survival, such as rent and health insurance for employees. These are clearly costs that need to be managed, and reduced, wherever possible. Last, there are those expenses that are actually investments. In other words, they produce a positive return over time—every dollar spent can be related to more than a dollar of revenue.

This is where the leverage in your business is—put one unit in, get more than one unit out. Marketing, sales, R&D, and less common areas like systemization and staff development all have the potential to produce enormous positive returns. This should be obvious to anybody who has looked at the numbers and the results, but it typically is not.

Spend More to Make More

Often the "budget," and therefore the spending for these items, is controlled by someone called a comptroller or an accountant or bookkeeper. All of these roles are associated with tracking and sometimes the reduction of the company's numbers, and the goal of these people is to keep things in line. Most of us think that you can keep more profits by reducing your expenses. That is only partially true. Of course, you have to manage expenses, especially those that are part of "overhead," and spend more in other areas to increase your total take.

The critical success areas in your company are always crying out for more cash. Areas like product development, lead generation, marketing, and sales force development are typically starved by arbitrary budget constraints imposed on the company for reasons that have nothing to do with growing your business.

Most business owners I meet with are financially cutting off their marketing departments at the knees. According to the U.S. Small Business Administration, most small businesses allocate around 2 percent of sales to fund their marketing. Contrast this with the incredibly profitable marketing juggernaut 1–800-Flowers, which spends more than 28 percent of revenues on marketing and sales, or the ubiquitous Adobe Systems, which has a healthy 23 percent operating profit while spending a whopping 33 percent on sales and marketing. This doesn't mean that you should spend more on marketing and sales—it depends on your exact business model—but almost certainly, you are spending too little.

Don't Base Business Decisions on Conventional Budgets

Don't get confused here; the goal is not to spend a certain percentage of your budget on a particular line item, although Wall

Street analysts and consultants selling "best practices" want you to do just that. Imagine looking over the fence into your neighbor's yard and deciding that you need a new swimming pool. Would you first find out how much he spent on the pool and divide that by his reported income? Then would you take the resulting percentage and apply it to your own earnings to calculate your pool budget?

No, you wouldn't. Yet that's exactly what analysts and best practices consultants want you to do: apply the collected wisdom of the companies in your competitive space (or, worse, your size range) and use that as the basis of your budget, without great regard for how well these other companies' marketing or their research or their staff programs perform.

A client with a training business has a very strong-willed comptroller who exerts undue influence over the budgeting process. The comptroller has successfully persuaded the board of directors that the company is spending too much on sales and marketing, based on the industry data she believes are appropriate. This advice is accepted, despite the fact that the company generates a significant return that is directly attributable to that spending, and the total return would surely be increased were the staff expanded. The unfortunate result is slowed company growth.

It may seem unreasonable to spend more than the collective wisdom dictates, but that is exactly what you should be doing if you want your company to grow faster than the market. The averages you benchmark against are producing *average* performance—how could it be otherwise? Consider this: the 2 percent that the Small Business Administration estimates for a marketing budget results in companies that on average last less than six years.

Superior Investment Strategy

Superior results, on the other hand, result from superior spending decisions. Not wasteful ones, to be sure, but from spending based on the distinction between expense and investment. Many companies consider investments to be those things that can be seen to persist over time, like land, buildings, capital equipment, and perhaps even research and development. This view is fostered by the securities markets, GAAP (Generally Accepted Accounting Principles), and the tax code. And while not incorrect, it is incomplete.

Consider anything that can produce a future return as an investment. While this definition includes the traditional investments, using this criterion, marketing and sales—building your customer base—can be the greatest investment of all. If $1 spent on marketing returns $5 this year, and $5 next year, and $5 the year after, shouldn't that be considered an investment? What about the training and development of your staff? Your CPA would probably not characterize that as an investment, preferring to label it an expense. But isn't the right training improving the performance of your team and the future profits that flow from it?

That's the unreasonable point of view. Transform your thinking about what is and isn't an expense so that you rethink your spending plan not only in sales and marketing, but everywhere that additional spending brings in additional returns.

Amar Bose spends all his profits (in other words, all the company's free cash—a huge amount by any standard) on research and product development. The result is a company that is second in market share to a company 50 times its size, and that is first in customer loyalty. And that market share and customer loyalty also translate into significantly higher margins. Best Buy, the electronics retailer, shifted its marketing approach from the traditional product focus to a more costly targeted customer focus, a unique and risky strategy that resulted in significant same-store sales growth (10 percent year over year) as well as a whopping jump in gross margins from 13.5 percent to 21 percent.

Many of today's large technology companies got there by spending as much as they could in two key areas: marketing and product development. Market domination requires that you gather lots and lots of customers, hopefully quickly. And it's not only happening in technology companies. Procter & Gamble spends more than 50 percent of the first year's revenue from a product on marketing and sales. Other packaged goods companies do the same. It's the only way to gain sufficient visibility and get customers in a crowded market. And software giant Microsoft spends about 21 percent of its revenues—and it's the market leader. If the market leader needs that much "push," how much will you need?

Your business may not require such drastic measures, but they are worthy of consideration. If you knew that you could generate $10 of sales for every $1 you spent, how much money would you spend? What if you could generate only $5? What if it was only $2? I ask this question often when I speak at conferences; my informal research always produces the same results: you'd spend all you could get your hands on! You'd borrow from the bank. You'd squeeze your investors. You'd mortgage your home and take money from the kids' college funds if it would make a difference. And then you'd figure out how to turn that 2 times into 5 times into 10 times. That's how unreasonable spending translates into extraordinary gains.

Extraordinary because the reasonable business executive will set a fixed percentage or a fixed amount for marketing and advertising and leave it at that, accepting whatever growth rate the market offers. And while normal companies spend 10 to 15 percent of their revenues on research and development, market dominators like Bose spend every free dollar available, because that is what keeps them out in front.

It's not only marketing and product development that benefit from extraordinary investment. Staff development is another overlooked area that's chock full of potential leverage. Best Buy profited from its well-trained and specially outfitted rapid-response "Geek Squad," and as part of its world-dominating strategy, coffee behemoth Starbucks invests more on staff development than any other company in its category. Starbucks trains its counter people—called baristas—in all the fine points of coffee products and processes, including the precise instructions for preparing a latte or a vanilla caramel Frappuccino. Baristas have the option of spending three months becoming "Coffee Masters," the true experts. Coffee Masters become outstanding promoters of the company and its products. This level of expertise, though costly at first blush, results in unprecedented customer loyalty and dramatically higher than average product margins.

Base your "investment" budgets on how much return you can generate for your company. Increase your spending on the things that are going to drive your business.

Companies can earn a lot more a lot faster by spending enough, and too many businesses fail because they don't have the guts to put their money—enough money—where their mouths are.

Just as important is your company's tolerance for mistakes, and for what other more reasonable people consider to be waste. Remember the old expression, "waste not, want not"? That seems like pretty good advice, but following it will kill off all hope of building an extraordinary business.

Are You Wasting Enough?

People who don't take risks generally make about two big mistakes a year.
People who do take risks generally make about two big mistakes a year.

—Peter Drucker, business writer and consultant

Smart companies figure out how to spend money to fuel their growth, and they tend to be careful about how much they're spending, often in an effort to maintain a certain level of profits. Of course, this makes perfect sense, but unreasonable companies have discovered something else. They've discovered the power of mistakes, and they've discovered the power of waste.

Standard operating procedure across the broad swath of businesses is to reward success, and to at best ignore, and at worst punish, failure. Why not? People who do the right things right and don't make mistakes produce more revenue at a lower cost. And that's good business. That's true, except that doing things well rarely results in a learning experience, and for the most part it can only perpetuate what has already been known to work. There is nothing bad about this—your company *does* want more revenue at a lower cost—and yet, if your company is to produce extraordinary results, you have to make mistakes and learn how to fix them.

Learn from Children

Watch a child learn anything—from walking, to putting a puzzle together, to talking, to riding a bike—and you realize that the way most children learn is by making lots of mistakes. Watch them try to walk. They stand up with the help of a nearby table, or the family dog. They let go. They fall down. Then they stand up again, and so on. A child will keep this up until she stops falling down; she's learned to walk, and at the same time she's learned something about self-reliance. Children do puzzles the same way: the pieces rarely go in correctly the first time, but eventually they learn how the pieces fit together—and, more important, they learn the process of fitting things together. Kids fall down on their two-wheelers, but eventually they learn how to stay up—and in the process, they learn about balance.

If you've watched an athlete train with a coach, you recognize the training as a process of making errors followed by subtle corrections leading to performance improvements. And anyone who's ever experienced the process of invention knows that this process is driven 100 percent by mistakes. It has to be; if the original worked OK, there would be no need for the new invention. Since it hasn't ever been done quite like this before, there is no model to do it right the first time. Imagine where we'd be if Edison had said, "OK, team. We've got five tries to get this right, and we'll use the best one."

Mistakes and the waste associated with them are an absolute requirement for learning, for performance improvement.

Waste Management

It's not just mistakes that need to be encouraged; sometimes you have to be willing to generate plain old waste to get the results you seek. Think of the direct mail model. Typical direct mail campaigns have a response rate—the percentage of envelopes or postcards that cause the recipient to take action—of between 0.25 and 2 percent. And 2 percent is considered a very good result. Imagine that—about 99 percent of the direct mail pieces that are sent out are wasted. In fact, a survey done by the U.S. Postal Service indicates that 65 percent of all mail doesn't even get opened! What tremendous waste. Does that mean no one should use direct mail as a marketing technique? Of course not—it just means that waste is part of the process.

Telemarketing is the same way. More than 50 percent of all calls result in hang-ups. Should you not make them? Don't stop—you should keep right on going, because all marketing is predicated on the fact that most of the messages you send out into the world result in failure, but the ones that succeed—if they succeed well—bring you great success. To my way of thinking, that means you have to be willing to "waste" even more.

What about hiring? In the insurance industry, two out of three new agents fail within the first year. Should you try to hire only the "good" ones? That won't work, because no one has figured out a way to accurately predict which new hires will go the distance.

This is the heart of the waste issue. Just as Edison couldn't tell ahead of time which filament would burn brightly enough for long enough, it is impossible (or at least prohibitively expensive) to figure out which mail piece, which recipient, which sales prospect, which new hire—which anything—is going to be the right one. Hence the nature of experimental trials, and hence the nature of productive waste in business.

There's another side to this, which is that when you try to screen your "candidates" too rigorously in an effort to prevent wasted effort, you can end up having too few people—or too few ideas—in your pipeline. That small number of candidates in itself can reduce both the volume and the velocity of your results. It is often more effective to be working on more possibilities in parallel than to try to eliminate costs and waste up front.

In the 1980s, Citibank had a policy in its systems development group that encouraged waste. Each important new project would launch multiple teams charged with the same task. The bank employed this strategy to create its first automated teller machines (ATMs), which revolutionized the banking world. The team that produced the most effective result was rewarded, and its solution lived on; the others were disbanded. Citibank used this same process externally as well. It would hire multiple consulting firms to develop a solution, managing the process with tight deliverables and checkpoints. At a certain point in the process, as soon as it could forecast the final outcome, it would pull the plug on the losers while the winners kept going.

To many this seemed like senseless, even arrogant waste, but since speed to market can translate into more immediate revenue and higher profit margins, this wasteful approach can earn superior returns. Citibank was the first to see the potential of automating a retail customer's interactions, and as a result of its crash programs, it had the first well-developed ATM network. The network gave Citibank a tremendous cost and service advantage, which it used to dominate the retail banking industry for a long time.

In fast-moving, innovative markets, where the first-mover advantage can translate into profits far in excess of the copycats', getting a solution into customers' hands before your competitors do can be the difference between success and failure. Potentially higher research and development costs, along with higher marketing costs, can turn into outsized profits. Don't get caught up in the argument about whether or not a first-mover advantage exists. It's not universal, but whenever your company has the chance to set a standard, or create a premier brand, or erect high barriers to entry, the resulting profits will exceed all expectations. And this result comes directly from being somewhere first. Slow and steady may keep costs down, but in the twenty-first century, it will not win the race. Waste wins!

Some businesses are built on significant amounts of waste, and there doesn't seem to be any other way to go about it. The semiconductor industry, which employs an unusually complex manufacturing process, expects between 10 and 30 percent of the manufactured wafers and chip devices to be bad. Many computational processes, like DNA sequencing, are all about waste. Slice up a section and see if it fits. If it does, great; but if it doesn't, slice up a new section, and so on.

Rapid prototyping is a way of getting a product to market faster. In rapid prototyping, a good-enough version that can satisfy the requirements is built and sold to "beta" customers. If it works, great; if not, you fix what's wrong and re-release it. The costs can be high, as rapid prototyping projects typically spend significantly more person-hours than a comparable linear design-build-test process. You may also "waste" customers, as a percentage of your beta buyers will be put off by bugs. But two important things happen. First, you get to market with something before your competitors, and you put a big stake in the ground that may be hard for them to dislodge. Second, you gain valuable intelligence on things such as consumer likes and dislikes, and which technology works and doesn't work. Yes, there is a lot of waste, but it breeds significant rewards that justify this unreasonable behavior.

Being willing to make mistakes and having deliberate waste are key parts of the creative process. Any attempt to minimize these will simply result in reduced creativity and reduced speed. Remember the great abstract expressionist painter Jackson Pollock. Pollock threw paint on his canvases in such a frenzy that more paint ended up on the studio floor than on the canvas, but his paintings today sell for tens of millions. What if Pollock had worried about wasting paint?

Breakdowns Lead to Breakthroughs

Just making mistakes is not the answer. You have to be willing to learn from them. And to learn from them, you have to be willing to celebrate them.

In cultures that punish errors, people try to hide their mistakes. You see this—or don't see it—in staff meetings all the time. No one ever raises his hand and says, "Things aren't working." Rarely do executives volunteer, "We're stuck, and we need help." It's not OK to be off track, and people go to great linguistic lengths to cover it up.

But what if you had a formal concept for stating that things weren't going as planned, that you were somehow off track, and that not only was it OK to bring up, it was an opportunity? Breakdowns are just that. They're not just any old failures; they are failures along the way while you are trying to get something done.

Let's say you open the garage door and you see that your car has a flat tire. There's nothing special about this. You do not call attention to it. You simply get it fixed. But how about if you are on your way to Grandma's, zipping along the freeway at 65 miles per hour, and all of a sudden . . . BLAM. That's something you call attention to. That's what philosopher Werner Erhardt called a breakdown.

A breakdown is an interruption in what you had planned. It's when things aren't working the way you thought they would; you've "tried everything," and you simply aren't getting the amount or quality of results that everyone counted on. Perhaps you are just off track. In any case, you make it formal. You're having a breakdown, and you want everyone to know about it.

Calling attention to a breakdown is being unreasonable, since in most organizations, we try to hide the fact that we're underperforming. Why would you make it public? When you try to hide your lack of results, either you ignore them yourself, or you attempt to fix the problem in secret. In either case, you're not bringing the full available resources to bear on the problem. But when you recognize and call attention to the fact that you are somewhat off track, you have the greatest opportunity to come up with a new solution set. You're making it clear that what you're doing is not working, and you are soliciting ideas.

This doesn't work in organizations where everyone is jockeying for advantage and power. In these places, it's all about looking good. No one calls attention to anything that has even a whiff of failure about it. In unreasonable companies, breakdowns become opportunities to call on the organization's full resources to help you.

Breakdowns are a way to go public and declare that you are actively searching for ways to improve your performance—to get back on track and deliver the goods as promised. You stand out there in the breeze soliciting help from all corners in the search for tweaks, twists, and turns to improve. You might even consider a totally fresh start.

On a psychological level, the very act of declaring a breakdown is liberating. You can stop trying to make the failing plan work when you're long past the point of believing that it can. Rather than trying to patch things up, breakdown thinking gives you the opportunity to declare the current approach dead and to review the initiative from scratch—or at least from the place where things started to go wrong. Formally declared breakdowns enable you to replan, retool, re-resource, and even reset your core assumptions, with the possibility of creating something more effective and more powerful than before. That's how breakdowns lead to breakthroughs.

Bill's company's software sales were dying. The software had a rich feature set, but it was technologically out of date, and the larger customers that Bill wanted to approach were shopping for a more powerful solution, as well as one that had a clearer future. The company responded by embarking on a new software development project to pave the way into the new market. About 12 months and several million dollars into the project, it realized that it would be another year and a half—or more—before the new system would be ready. In the meantime, the traditional customer base, under pressure of a recession, had stopped buying the existing product, and the company was on the ropes. Not only was the software dying, so was the company. At first it simply sold harder, but after a time everyone realized that this wasn't going to work. Instead of trying to "fix things" while looking good, the people at the company cried out for help. With a collective sigh and great clarity, they realized that the product on which they'd built the company was effectively dead and that they were not going to sell any more of it. The time-honored remedies—better marketing and better sales—weren't going to make a difference, and patching on a few new features wasn't going to help either. The owners were exhausted, and they considered closing up shop, thinking that that might be the best resolution to their current situation. But a funny thing happened: out of this realization that they could walk away from the whole thing came a new sense of freedom.

So Bill declared a formal breakdown, stating that the old ways of doing business were no longer productive, and that the company had to reinvent its business—immediately. During an all-hands offsite meeting, the company decided to respond to the breakdown by shifting the company's focus and transforming it into a service organization, mobilizing all marketing, sales, and available technologists to provide professional services to the aging—and financially hard-pressed—customer base. The recession that made it hard for customers to make capital expenditures was tailor-made for people selling short-term performance enhancers. The customers loved it, and the company flourished.

Beware. The formal announcement that you don't know what you are doing—a key part of the breakdown/breakthrough strategy—can lead to high levels of frustration. People who don't understand what you're doing will think that their jobs, even their careers, are at risk. Expect to see finger pointing and fault finding. If the strategy is poorly managed, there will be lots of blame, accusations, and hostility. And breakdowns create chaos. You've just declared what everyone has been thinking all along: the things that used to work aren't working anymore, and it's all up for grabs. Roll with it—that's what you wanted to do. It is that state of chaos that gives you the greatest possibility to break through. Let everyone know that that is the plan. Take collective responsibility for the situation and declare that victory is in sight.

Being unreasonable embraces a school of thought that says that if you are not making mistakes, wasting enough, and experiencing breakdowns on a regular basis, you cannot possibly be maximizing the potential of your company. You are playing it safe, you are sticking with the things that you know will work, and as a result you are underperforming on your potential. Unreasonable performance takes guts and the willingness to leave safety behind. Unreasonable performers don't exactly court failure, but they are willing to fail in order to succeed.

The Unexamined Mistake Is Not Worth Making

With all apologies to Socrates, just making mistakes is an idiot's game. Keep making mistakes without learning from them and you will find yourself out of business, fast. To surge your business forward, you must consider your mistakes in the cold light of the aftermath. You have to conduct the postmortem. What went wrong? Why did it happen? What was missing? What needs to be changed? What could be added? What could be done differently?

The postmortem requires critical thinking. "I don't know" is an OK place to begin, but it is unacceptable as a final answer. Thinking is the process of *asking and answering questions*, and these questions must be answered if you are to make any progress. Dig in deep and figure it out so that your business profits from what didn't work and works better the next time. Not perfectly, perhaps, but definitely better.

Notice that none of these questions addresses the question of who did what or who is to blame. As soon as you try to pin it on someone, you will shut down innovation and progress. If you recognize innovation that succeeds while punishing experiments that fail, you will crush creativity. Auto manufacturer BMW has a formal program that actually rewards mistakes and encourages risk taking. Managers at eBay have public forums where they have to explain what they did right, wrong, and very wrong. Formal programs, such as "Mistake of the Month," that encourage employee experimentation are strong signals that it's OK to go out on the edge.

Get the Minority Report

In Philip K. Dick's 1956 short story "Minority Report," violent crimes that have not yet happened are forecast by three genetically altered "precogs," short for precognitive. The precog-predicted perpetrators are apprehended before the deeds take place, leading to the complete eradication of murder and mayhem. Of course, this type of system could be dangerous, so to prevent wrongful arrest, they work in a three-precog team. All three precogs are supposed to agree, because they aren't predicting; they are looking at the future. From time to time, however, there is a *minority report*, where one of the three precogs sees the future differently. One such minority report is suppressed by a municipal official, and that sets this story in motion.

It's a useful idea, the minority report. Unreasonable people—those acting outside what normal people consider normal—often generate those reports. But like the fictional government of Dick's story, the minority report is often suppressed, either by management or by the reporters themselves. After all, who wants to be publicly in disagreement with everyone else?

Encourage the minority report to come out. You don't have to act upon it, but you do want to take it into consideration. The minority report can be a rich source of outlying opinion, of contrary thinking, of deviant ideas. Make sure you are able to tap into this vein of unreasonableness.

Next comes a little-discussed suite of business tactics that can revolutionize every aspect of your company. Systems are not sexy and they don't make headlines. But a well-systemized business is set to take off like a rocket ship.

Blame the System

If a team member is failing, sometimes blaming that individual seems like the reasonable thing to do. After all, it is her action, her results, her accountability. Someone has to take the fall, right?

No, not right. Poor performance may be caused by a fault in the system rather than by someone's incompetence or mistake. This is not meant to allow your people to duck responsibility—they are the ones who are supposed to make the system work. But if the programs and processes that you've laid down are not up to the job, do you really want to punish the people who run them? If the bell is mute, do you blame the bell ringer? Of course not; you fix the bell.

Bad or even missing systems are at the heart of a lot of subpar and inconsistent performance. Argue as you may about whether or not you like McDonald's hamburgers, they are always the same. As are the French fries, the fish sandwiches, the shakes, all of it. Well-run franchise systems all have one thing in common: an operating system that defines in detail how things are to be done.

Learn from the Big Systems

The key to Operations at Wal-Mart is their ability to maintain the highest standards while at the same time getting things done with lockstep execution.

—Michael Bergdahl, author of *What I Learned from Sam Walton*

McDonald's has an operations and training manual that is thousands of pages long. Starbucks's coffee manual for baristas is four inches thick. Parmasters Golf Training Centers has 2,300 pages of operations and training binders. Companies that plan to grow big define processes and document systems for every essential and minor operation in their company. Quantum Growth Consulting has defined 88 essential business processes and created step-by-step systems for each one. This obsessive organization and attention to detail results in what the franchise world calls duplication, the ability to have the job done well, the same way, every time.

The beauty of documented systems is (and this is true even if your business has only one location) once they have been tested, following your systems results in consistent, predictable, and continually improving business performance. The converse of this is that when you have consistently bad performance, you often have either bad systems or no systems.

It's the difference between ad hoc and rigor. Creative types typically like to do things ad hoc. They like to make things up as they go, always pushing the bounds and exploring new territory. They don't like to write things down and be stuck with any one way of doing something. So for these people, perhaps the most unreasonable thing you can do is expect them to figure something out, then lock it down. Add rigor and predictability to the process.

Predictability? Isn't that a bit too reasonable?

It's not predictability that's bad; predictability in systems is great. Being a slave to predictability is what's bad. Acting predictably in an unpredictable world is what's dangerous. We encourage repetition and consistency, at least for a while. Once you get the hang of how to do something so that it works, keep at it until you discover a better way. Don't worry, someone will slip up and make a mistake, and sometimes that mistake will improve the program. Go with it. Or the boys in the lab will hit upon something. Run with it.

Keep it up until the outside world shifts sufficiently that performance suffers. Then you figure out what's wrong and make the change. You evolve.

So when an employee's results go bad, find out if it's the person or the process. If you don't have any documentation, then you know where to fix the fault. If you have developed that three-ring binder, find out whether your people are following it. Are they checking off the checklists? Are the steps being performed with rigor? Do you even have a way to find out? If the system is being adhered to and you aren't getting the expected results, then the system is definitely to blame.

Systems Themselves Are Unreasonable

You ask what is the use of classification, arrangement, systemization?
I answer you: order and simplification are the first steps toward the
mastery of a subject—the actual enemy is the unknown.

—Thomas Mann

People have two reactions when we talk about systemizing their businesses. Either they think it's a horrible idea that will upset their people and cause them to want to quit, or they think that systemizing would be a great idea, but it will just be too hard.

Systemization is a paradox. Systems instill rigor, standardization, and rationality into your business. You would expect that such "regularization" would mean that the business would settle into a boring routine and produce modest yet predicable profits. Yet the outcome of building a business based on systemization can be nothing short of a total breakthrough. Three of my favorite unreasonable companies, Southwest Airlines, Dell Computer, and FedEx, are companies that have grown on the backs of deeply entrenched systems.

Having well-developed systems is like imprinting the corporate DNA; they make it almost impossible for anyone to copy your business, and in each of these three cases, no one has. Southwest's corporate DNA is an interlocking set of well-thought-out systems—each of which is distinct from its competitors'. It doesn't transfer baggage; it has never served food; its boarding passes are simplified As, Bs, and Cs; it flies only 737s to reduce training and maintenance costs; and it pays its people bonuses for fast gate turnaround. Its reservation system is easy to use, and because the flights are not tied into the big ticketing systems like Sabre and Gemini, it saves on sales costs, plus there's the added benefit of making it difficult for travelers to compare costs. In every visible choice, Southwest has engineered itself from the ground up to be the low-cost efficient airline. Amazingly, it has done this without sacrificing quality and has continually ranked at the top in customer satisfaction. Where other airlines' cost-cutting measures anger customers, Southwest, because it has always been cheap, has trained its passengers to enjoy the cheap structure. It's crafted an exquisitely systemized culture around this structure; it's even systemized having fun. And without starting from scratch and reverse engineering the whole thing, Southwest's systemized success cannot be duplicated.

The other paradox of systemization is that while people believe that systems are the death knell for creativity, the opposite is actually true. Systemized companies standardize the routine, relieving people's minds of trying to figure it out each and every day. Instead of focusing on the commonplace, people's minds are free to consider the extraordinary. Creativity soars.

Having systems frees your people in another way too. In a reasonable environment, people learn a job and become stuck in it. But imagine what would happen if everyone in your business were disposable and mobile. When all the processes and procedures are standardized and documented, all workers have the same ability to do the job well—and they'd better, because you can easily replace them. At the same time, they are all free to move around more easily, because the documented systems make it easy for other people to perform the job. Any job. When you have adequately systemized your business to the point where anyone can perform any job, you have given yourself a very special freedom that only a few businesses can boast. You are in a position to take drastic action.

Fire Your Superstars

Superstars are the uniquely talented individuals who intuitively create results by doing things their own way. That sounds like just what the doctor ordered, doesn't it? Unreasonably effective and willing to do it outside the bounds—great! Yes, true—but there's one problem. These people insist on doing it their way, not yours. And true superstars, just like operatic prima donnas, always get their way.

Superstars always perform; that's what they're built for. If they don't perform, they're not superstars. Performance is what gives them their star quality, their identity, and it's easy to think that superstar performance is exactly what you want. But because superstars want to do it their way and not yours, there is a significant risk in basing your success on them.

Jack ran a company that sold automated health-care solutions for regional hospitals. The company had a superstar salesperson, Warren, who was a certified high performer and sold the lion's share of the company's aging product line. The product's "green screen" interface made it decreasingly competitive, and sales had slipped to the point where none of the other salespeople were selling anything. Not only was Warren the star producer, he was the only producer. As a stopgap measure, I recommended changing the price structure to include an automatic upgrade to an as-yet-unannounced new version with a generous service package. I hoped that this move would increase the value proposition sufficiently to keep the company afloat while it readied the new product for launch. My client resisted this approach.

"Why?"

"Warren won't like it."

Huh?

"Warren won't like it. He's happy with the way things are."

My dumbfounded response: "So?"

"Well, if Warren doesn't like it, he'll stop selling, and that would be the end for us."

You see, "your" superstars aren't really playing on your team. They're on their own team—the all-star team. And while they definitely pay their way, sooner or later—like all reasonable solutions—your superstars stop performing. At which point you're in big trouble. When, after finally wising up, you try to mitigate the situation by hiring other salespeople, shifting the product mix, introducing new marketing—anything that changes the game and may diminish their superstar standing—they balk. They threaten to walk. Most entrepreneurs cave in. The superstars you fell in love with have just put a hammerlock on your future.

Conventional wisdom loves superstars. The idea is to find a bunch of them and ride them to build your company. I know a sales trainer and management consultant who promotes a strategy designed to attract star salespeople, as if you could repeatedly find them. That's like believing Garrison Keillor when he says, "All the children in Lake Wobegon are above average." It's pretty hard to find a group of superstars because of the regression to the mean effect.

Everything does have a time and a place, and superstars have theirs. They're great for launching a business or rescuing a turnaround. In both cases, superstars provide much-needed cash to run the business while you do something smart. Just don't bet your future on them. There is one other great use for superstar performers, whether it's star salespeople or star anything. Transform what's in their heads into bona fide intellectual property. Cast them as role models and use their habits and skills as the basis for creating a system that can be duplicated. Find out what they do well, and in what sequence. Discover exactly what they say, how they write, what they think, what they believe, what they do when, and document everything. Audiotape them. Videotape them. Transcribe everything. Figure out what makes them tick. Then teach that to other people in the same role and watch performance soar. Be sure you don't limit your modeling activities to externals. The internals—mindset, belief system, self-image, self-talk—are as important as, if not more important than, what you see on the outside.

Your superstars may balk at first, so you'll probably have to flatter them into it. That's fine, because you know that one day there will come a clash of wills, and they'll choose to bolt. Before that time comes, you want to download their "wetware" and put it on a hard drive. When you've proven that the system works—that other people can approximate their stellar results—the job is done.

W. Edwards Deming, the American statistician who is considered to be the father of modern Japanese manufacturing, espoused a philosophy summarized as "raise the mean and reduce the standard deviation." By downloading your superstars' methods and uploading them into your average performers, you'll have done just that. You've just raised the averages of your average performers. Don't worry if the regular performers aren't quite up to the performance of the superstars. You've done something unreasonable, which is that you have beat the odds. You can find more "previously average" performers—which is a whole lot easier and less risky than recruiting superstars—and reliably make them better. You've achieved Deming's goal.

Superstars boast because they can, and their boastful natures are often part of their success strategies. For the most part, the rest of us do not boast, and it may be to our detriment. The next set of tactics is about developing that boastful nature and putting it to amazing use.

The Magic of Unreasonable Claims

As children, we're repeatedly told not to boast. Why? There are a few reasons. It may be a concern for our safety. Boasting draws attention to us, and once people know that we're there, they can attack us. Or it may go back to the Reformation. The New Testament says, "Come and do your boasting in the Lord," and both Puritans and Quakers expressly forbade sartorial finery and anything that smacked of calling attention to oneself. Or farther back than that. Saint Augustine wrote that "pride is the commencement of all sin," And boasting is the announcement of pride.

Whatever the source, prohibitions against boasting are deeply rooted in many cultures. However, there's nothing wrong with making big, unreasonable claims, as long as you can back them up. Such claims, in fact, can bolster your leadership position and make you famous.

What's unreasonable about an unreasonable claim is that first, a reasonable person wouldn't say such a thing, and second, the claim itself may be beyond the bounds of reason. Similarly, unreasonable claims have a dual effect. First, they call attention to the claimants—some would say the boasters—and if they pull it off, that attention may gather publicity and all sorts of other benefits that they couldn't buy otherwise. The second effect is rather different.

Unreasonable claims have the effect of putting a giant stake in the ground. When you make your big, fat claim loudly and publicly enough, you are committed. No two ways about it. You have told the world what you intend to do, and, just like Cortez's army after he so famously burned the boats, retreat is cut off. You have left yourself without any choice.

After only a brief introduction to the principles of the psychological techniques of Neuro-Linguistic Programming, Anthony Robbins took the technique on the road, appearing on radio and television stations throughout Canada and the United States to tout the wonders of this new "technology of change." A natural showman, he was so confident of his ability to induce dramatic change in people that he began to publicly challenge psychiatrists, asking for a chance to work with their toughest cases in front of a live audience. On national television, he was presented with a woman who had a paralyzing fear of snakes that had so far resisted seven years of psychotherapy. Robbins cured the woman of her snake phobia in only 15 minutes, garnering press throughout the world and launching his stupendous career.

Robbins's claim was unreasonable, but he made good on it. Robbins's friend, real estate guru Robert Allen, used a similar approach when he made a public bet on *Larry King Live*. He said that his negotiation and "no money down" real estate strategies were so good that you could drop him off anywhere in the United States without any money in his pocket and he would own seven properties within 48 hours. The *Los Angeles Times* took Allen up on the bet. Within 48 hours, not only had he secured the seven properties—all for no money down—but he had secured his national reputation.

Allen and Robbins made big, bold, unreasonable claims. They didn't focus on what was likely to happen; that would be a big yawn—nobody would care. They focused on the unreasonable, and everyone was betting that they would lose. For both of them, not only was the outcome possible, but in their minds it was a given.

Biotech leader J. Craig Venter boasted that he would beat the federally funded Human Genome Project and be the first to decode the human DNA sequence. Venter's claims earned him heaps of scorn from the academic community, and many questioned his methods, but depending on how you look at it, he did get there first.

Not all big claims are brags, and the power of an unreasonable claim to move people is well documented. Consider John F. Kennedy's famous declaration that the United States would have a man on the moon by the end of the 1960s. The United States moved heaven and earth to reach that goal, and in the process transformed key components of education and industry in this country.

Unreasonable claims inspire people to action. We get caught up in the grandeur of the idea; that's why the claim works. Small ideas rarely move anyone to action—small risk, small reward, the saying goes—and small ideas can't move people far enough to get anything interesting to happen. But outsized claims that don't quite seem impossible can energize a team and get it moving.

People worry about how they will get something done. Don't. Focus on the what; get everyone excited around that. Then figure out the how. The how always comes, and it's much easier to develop the how when you have more minds engaged and more resources to play with.

Anyone who's ever raised money for a start-up company knows that it's often easier to raise a million dollars—even two million— than it is to raise $250,000. The small amount isn't enough to get anyone excited; there isn't sufficient return. But the larger amounts might just pay back tenfold, and wouldn't that be something. Of course, to raise more money, you have to make larger claims—often unreasonable claims—and then work like the dickens to deliver on them.

The bigger the claim, and the more publicly it is made, the more attention you will get. Inside your company, people will take potshots at your idea. Bring it on, you say, because it is just that interaction you want. Get them to help you debug your idea, pointing out what's wrong and figuring out how to make it right. Make that claim. Make it lively. Make it public.

Call it the drive to succeed. Call it commitment. Call it discipline. No matter what you call it, the next tactic is something usually associated with a personality trait, not a business process. Don't make the mistake of thinking that it is something that you must be born with. It is powerful, perhaps the most powerful thing you can bring to your company and the people in your company. Used properly, it will affect your business more than any group of marketing and sales tactics you can think of. You can build your own, and you can do it deliberately.

Taking the Longer View

Most salespeople can't wait to get in and pitch their wares. That's what's expected of them, and for the most part that's what they're inclined to do. Jeff Walker is different. His specialty is launching new products with an unreasonable method. Essentially he builds a relationship with his market, teasing them with tidbits of information and small pieces of value until they crave the product or service he still hasn't offered.

"When I look at my business—an online business that sells information—the thing that has set me apart is that I have always focused, first and foremost, on creating relationships with my prospects long before I try to sell them something. So many times people can't wait to go for the jugular; personally, I'd rather build a relationship first. Whatever it is, whether it's writing copy, sending out e-mails, Web pages—whatever—I'm always striving to create the relationship, deepen the relationship, and then—and only then—go for the sale. A lot of people consider me unreasonable, and it's because most people aren't willing to take the long view. They prefer immediate gratification. They want results now. They want them yesterday. This need for immediacy affects so many people, and it keeps them from getting what they really want.

"People who take the long view win. Look at Warren Buffett. He's completely unreasonable when you compare him to other investors. He says, 'I don't care about the trends; if I don't understand it, I'm going to skip it.' For me—it's about taking the long term in developing a relationship with my prospect, and I'm willing to work with it until it bears fruition. Like Buffett, I'm taking an incredibly long view. I can do this because I know it will work; I just have to be willing to hold on until it does.

"I've been willing to take the long view: treating people right, never compromising my ethics, and it's paying off. I really believe in the Golden Rule—treat people like you want to be treated, and it's all about worrying about my relationships—for the long term. For the long haul. What's great about this approach is that it's so grounded in human nature that it works for almost anybody, with any kind of personality and any kind of business. Hundreds of companies have used my 'Product Launch Formula' system to successfully launch new products and services.

"Here's how it's worked for me. As I said a moment ago, my business is about publishing information, and I've been selling products on the Internet for about 10 years. Four years ago I decided I might want to teach others how to do what I do. I began by setting up a Web site collecting e-mail names and establishing a presence. I wasn't sure where it was going, but I did what I know how to do: I created relationships with my readers, established a presence, and developed a toehold. I finally did get noticed, and when I launched my training and teaching business, it just exploded. It's crazy to me, but in 1995 I was setting goals for my annual income, and I've earned more money in a single hour than I set as a yearly goal 12 years ago. That's the unreasonable power of the long view."

Will Is a Four-Letter Word

In war, the chief incalculable is the human will.

—Sir Basil Liddell Hart

Because there is nothing more destructive than making boastful, outrageous claims in public that you can't back up, be sure you carry them out. If you've made a really unreasonable claim—one that couldn't possibly have been true at the time you made it—then you have a lot of work ahead of you. To turn your claims into reality is going to require something that is alien to most people: *application of the will*. Willpower means taking action regardless of whether you feel like it. Will is the ability to keep going no matter what, often because you know it'll be good for you, and other times simply because you said you would.

So much of people's time in organizations is just plain wasted—diffused and lacking power like scattered sunlight. Work time is squandered and unfocused, and the 8 to 10 hours a day that people are physically present results in much less than that amount of useful service. A few years ago, we conducted a survey to determine how much of the workday was perceived as productive. Over and over, managers and executives said that they averaged 1 to 2 hours of really productive time. I share that figure when I speak with groups of executives, and they typically howl in response. I originally thought people were insulted; now I realize the number I'm quoting is too high!

Will, properly applied, can change all that. Will has the power to transform ordinary existence into something truly remarkable. Having a strong will goes hand in glove with making unreasonable claims—you can promise bold things when you're convinced that you have the steel to follow through. Having a strong will is behind every unreasonable request. You ask with conviction, knowing that if the tables were reversed, you'd be able to say yes and mean it.

Obsessively Create Value: An Unreasonable Case Study

When I was growing up I wanted to be a rock star, but I didn't get the goods. I didn't have the musical ear, I didn't have the rock star looks, and I couldn't really play. But I still wanted to provide impact and value for tons of people, so I decided to be an entrepreneur.

—Chris Knight, CEO and Publisher of EzineArticles

One way to ensure client loyalty is to obsessively create value for them. While this should seem obvious, most business owners don't act like it is. (*Most unreasonable tactics seem so obvious as to be almost not worth mentioning, except that very few people are using them.*) Many entrepreneurs realize that they need to create value for their clients, but they do it in measured amounts. They create value relative to what they are being paid, and they feel they should do just that much and no more.

Chris Knight is an Internet entrepreneur running one of the most popular sites on the Internet. The core of his site, EzineArticles.com, is providing articles that readers and other Web site publishers can use free of charge. In a record amount of time, he has assembled more free high-quality content than any competitor. Knight took over and relaunched EzineArticles.com a little over two years ago, and as of this writing, it is approximately the 700th most popular site on the Web. If you didn't know better, you might say, "Seven hundredth? That's not that popular," but out of more than 10 million Web sites, that's quite an accomplishment. How did he go from almost none to over 250,000 visitors each day?

"I have a belief that the amount of money you make is proportional to the amount of value you create," says Knight, "My objective is to create massive amounts of value for a massive amount of people. It's all about service to others; that's how I accomplish my personal goals."

The entire business is grounded in finding out how to provide that massive value and great service. Much of the value is in the size of the content base: EzinArticles.com offers more free articles than any other article distribution site, which makes it a wonderful resource for authors seeking distribution and for publishers seeking content. It is growing faster as well. Because available content management software didn't provide an acceptable user experience, the company built its own—not a small undertaking. Version 1.0 wasn't up to Knight's concept of value, so the company began soliciting visitor feedback and applying it in a process of never-ending improvement. "Our users are like our board of directors," Knight proclaims. He urges other infopreneurs to allow users to create the future of their own experience, building visitor returns. The value that EzineArticles.com provides is not derived from any one piece, but is made up of hundreds of tiny improvements to its end-to-end process, made each week as a result of user suggestions.

How else does this value obsession play out? The company measures everything: page load times, end-user response times, numbers of errors, uptime. It follows the "small planet theory": with EzineArticles.com's extreme level of traffic, there aren't many slipups that happen without someone complaining. Which means that the obsession with value is also an obsession with quality.

The company feels the same way about the content itself. From an editorial perspective, the articles are about tips and techniques. EzineArticles.com doesn't see itself as an advocate of citizen journalism, and the business is not about free speech. What that means is that human editors remove all offensive content before it gets published, and editorial complaints are dealt with immediately. While Knight has great respect for his authors, there is no single writer on the site that the company thinks would be worth trading viewers for.

All of this would be unreasonable enough—this company goes above and beyond its competitors in every single dimension, which is how it has outstripped them and outmarketed them. But the company has a philosophy that is at its core unreasonable. It can be summed up in two words: go deep. EzineArticles.com has succeeded by having the will to go deeper than anyone else will reasonably go. It has deeper technical expertise, it has deeper analysis of its own operations, and it has deeper content. Knight says, "True mastery can't be had until you have gone deeper than anyone else. Only then can you call yourself the master."

Will Building

The big secret in life is that there is no big secret. Whatever your goal, you can get there if you're willing to work.

—Oprah Winfrey

The will is like a muscle; the more you train it, the stronger it gets. Everyone in your company has some level of muscle tone, and everyone has some willpower. If you haven't been to the gym in years and don't engage in regular exercise, you are probably pretty weak. If you haven't spent any time exercising your will, it is probably weak as well.

The way to build will is simple. You use it. The best way is to set tasks that are just outside your abilities, that require greater focus, attention, and persistence, and then get them done. The secret is doing things with forethought and by design. It doesn't do much will building to accomplish things by accident. You must decide that you're going to do something at a certain time and with certain conditions of satisfaction, and then do it. That builds the will. Then you decide to do something else that's a bit beyond your grasp, and you do that. More will. Over time, your ability to intend results and produce them is transformed. Instead of being like diffuse sunlight, your will acts as a laser beam: focused and coordinated and capable of great power.

Start the way beginning bodybuilders build muscle tone. They begin with a weight that they can lift but that exerts a strain, perhaps 25 pounds. They repeat that until it is no longer difficult, and then they move up to 30 pounds. They continue with that until it becomes easy, and then they move up again. After a time they're lifting hundreds of pounds. You can build your organizational will the same way.

Start with something small. It doesn't really matter what it is—it could be making a commitment to call a client at exactly 3:15 p.m. or visiting your gym for that long-needed exercise today at 6:30 a.m. sharp. Perhaps it's sending a new business letter you've been putting off, or having one-on-ones with your team this week, no matter what. For some people it's as elementary as getting to the office at a fixed time or starting and stopping meetings exactly on schedule. Begin anywhere; tell whomever you need to tell, and do it.

Take it to the next level. What recurring item do you typically start, then stop? What's something that you want to do every week, but never do for more than two weeks in a row? It could be those one-to-ones. That's what ordinary people do—they start, then they stop. But those with willpower simply decide. Then they do.

Pick one of those stop-start-stop-start things, put it on your schedule, and do it. You don't have to commit forever; you can commit for the next four weeks. When you're done, commit again. Go to the gym every day at the same time, 6:30 a.m., for the next four weeks. Each and every day, each and every week. And do it. Each time you decide and do, you are reinforcing and strengthening the power of your will. Make it through the next four weeks, and you can recommit and add something else. Over the course of time, you'll build up a huge reservoir of power. Building your will is incremental, but the effect is cumulative, and ultimately you reach the tipping point where your will has an almost unbelievable effect on your business's ability to produce results.

Get your team members involved as well. Talk to them about will and have them make small decisions. Then bigger ones. Then big ones.

There is one thing that will hamper the development of the will, and that is fooling around with the truth—anything from out-and-out lying to exaggerating or stretching the truth, even "puffery" and "loose interpretations." Of course, this is just good business sense; stick to the facts, and everything will work out. But in developing your will, the truth works, and everything that's not the truth works against you.

In *The Most Famous Man in America*, Debby Applegate reports that when Henry Ward Beecher was asked how he could accomplish so much more than others, he replied, "I don't do more, but less than other people. They do all their work three times. Once in anticipation, once in actuality, and once in rumination. I do mine in actuality alone, so I end up doing things just once." Beecher had the ability to concentrate his mind and focus his will on what he was doing at the moment, to the exclusion of all else. He applied his will to the problems before him; this gave him great productivity and power.

Normal people seem unable to do this. They allow themselves to get distracted by whatever seems interesting or demanding at the moment, whether it's an e-mail ding, a ringing phone, or a colleague come to discuss last night's game or the recent heat wave. After all, it's reasonable to pay attention to people when they're right in front of you, isn't it? Or to answer the phone when it rings—that's what we've all been taught. It may be reasonable, but it isn't going to help much.

In the 1980s and 1990s, the trend in office design was to eliminate the traditional four walls in favor of movable partitions and open floor space. Besides being cheaper to implement and providing more flexibility, there was a popular notion that it was more egalitarian, that it flattened the organization, and that it helped executives be closer to the pulse of things. But according to a survey of 1,500 employees by the English recruiting firm Office Angels, more than three-quarters of Britons complain that open-plan working environments not only stifle their creativity but also hamper their ability to get the job done. Among other things, 84 percent of them want closed-door offices, and 8 out of 10 find it generally difficult to focus in an open-plan environment. It seems that the willpower of the majority of office workers is not up to the task of putting interruptions in the background.

The art of being unreasonable depends to a large extent on a well-developed will, much like Henry Ward Beecher's. Applied will is part of the puzzle; the other part is the discipline of regularity. Think again of our beginning weight lifter. It does no good to show up at the gym at 6:30 in the morning three days in a row and then not return for weeks. Muscle building can't happen that way. Neither can weight loss. Try eating right for one week. Great, but then what happens? Nothing. In fact, worse than nothing. Disappointment sets in because the expected results don't materialize.

It's the same thing with any execution program. Most marketing programs fail because companies don't have the discipline to execute them month after month. Sales programs fail because the salespeople don't execute day in and day out. Staff meetings happen for a few weeks until everyone gets busy, and then they get dropped. To succeed, each of these programs requires company will and discipline so that each is executed repeatedly for as long as it takes to produce the expected results. Will to do it in the first place; discipline to keep it going, over and over, until it's no longer needed.

Once you've forged your collective company will, you will surely feel the need to make tough choices between one set of resources and another, between one set of tactics and another. All of the items on your menu may look appealing, and they may all seem like terrific options. And so they may be, but that doesn't mean that you can have them all. Being able to choose and choose well is a hallmark of maturity.

Sacrifice Means Never Having to Say You're Sorry

> *It is not what we take up, but what we give up, that makes us rich.*
>
> —Henry Ward Beecher

In my role as advisor to CEOs, people often ask me, "How should I prioritize my time?" My first answer typically begs the question: "Do what is going to have the biggest impact." Relative to what? To everything you are striving for.

What is going to have the biggest impact on realizing your vision, on achieving your mission and your strategic goals, on reaching your monthly profit targets? Figure out what is most important about your business, and then figure out what is going to have the biggest impact on achieving that.

Normal people quite reasonably spend their energy on what they think other people expect them to focus on. Unreasonable people laser in on the things that are going to rock their world. Customers call, and you are supposed to jump. After all, it makes sense to keep the customers happy. But what if you are in the last crucial stages of launching a campaign that will double your business overnight? Should you take that call?

Sacrifice means giving up something of value for something of even greater value. It doesn't mean dumping the insignificant things; sacrifice asks which among the meaningful things is most meaningful, and lets go of the rest. Perhaps temporarily, perhaps forever. Sacrifice is the tool of the unreasonably committed. Knowing that you are going to achieve your outcomes no matter what, you decide what will get you there faster and what will hold you back.

People talk about opportunity cost; it's a question of sacrifice. If your company chooses to develop product A, it may mean that there are no resources available to pursue product B. And that may cost you. If you decide to woo customer X, then customers Y and Z may suffer. See? Trade-offs. Sacrifices.

Beecher said it brilliantly: it's what we give up that makes us rich. Companies that target well—their products, their markets, their customers—often have to give up other lucrative opportunities. It works the same way in your personal life. It's hard to be both a lawyer and a doctor—especially at the same time. Want to be an astronaut? You may have to forgo that career as a singer. Sacrifices have to be made. Airlines do this all the time when they drop marginal routes to focus on more profitable ones. It's not that the routes are worthless; they may even be profitable, but there aren't enough planes to cover them all.

Corporations do this when they sell divisions. IBM recently sold its entire laptop division to Chinese computer giant Lenovo. The laptop division was profitable, and ThinkPad remains one of the most respected brands in the business, but the product line was no longer consistent with IBM's future direction, and management resources were needed to run other parts of the company. The company sacrificed ThinkPad and gave up a profitable revenue stream for greater gain elsewhere.

Unreasonable requests are not satisfied out of thin air. There is no magic that creates 26-hour days or 9-day weeks. The magic of unreasonable requests derives from grabbing people's attention and focusing it on your objectives and programs while turning it away from whatever else they were doing. That "whatever else" may have also been valuable, and thus something is going to get sacrificed. It's important to understand sacrifice, especially when you get pushback. There is always going to be an opportunity cost. The question you have to ask is, does that matter to you? It may not. The lost opportunity may be trivial—more time spent checking e-mail doesn't count for much. Or the lost opportunity may be *someone else's* opportunity, and that loss goes on her expense statement, not yours.

Many consider *sacrifice* to be a dirty word, and that concern stops many reasonable people from making hard decisions. Not wanting to let go of something good stands in the way of your company's ability to focus. Your unreasonable request coupled with a strong will to carry things through can change all that. Once you get the hang of choosing one thing over another, one of the first things you can sacrifice is relativism.

Seeing the World in Black and White

In earlier times, people saw the world in terms of opposites: black or white, good or evil, weak or strong, success or failure, profit or loss, win or lose, in or out, right or wrong, friend or foe, ally or competitor, with us or against us.

In the last 50 years, however, it has become fashionable to see the world in terms of shades of gray. Instead of making definite judgments about people and things, the world has moved to points on a continuum, and most evaluations have become relative. Shades of gray is now the reasonable way to look at things.

This is not necessarily bad. Many things in our world defy categorization, and many situations are not wholly one way or another. Putting things in terms of black and white requires you to make firm distinctions where there may not be any. But some issues *are* cut and dried: profit is good; loss is bad. Friends are good; enemies are bad. High quality and low product returns are good; low quality and unsatisfied customers are bad. And so on.

The difficult part of this is that calling things black or white creates polarization; some people are included in your worldview, and others are excluded. Some things fit your model, and others do not. It is unreasonable to express unequivocal values and ask people to take a stand. It is unreasonable to draw a line in the sand and ask people to cross it.

Why make such harsh distinctions? Why risk alienating half your potential supporters, half your team, half your marketplace? Why, indeed? Because in the marketplace and in the workplace, people seek bold leadership. *They want to take a stand. They want to embrace a vision. They want life to mean something, and they want to be passionate about something.* And wishy-washy relativism kills off passion and meaning, and people are tired of it. So what if you polarize your constituents? The ones who join with you and follow you are the ones you want anyway. Sure, you'll lose the rest, but you would probably never have won them in the first place.

Make no mistake, this is very strong medicine, and it is one of the most dynamic tactics in this book. Choosing to act along black-and-white lines will alter the fortunes of your business. Unreasonably so.

Pain Is a Given

Pain is a given. All suffering is optional.

—Anonymous Zen aphorism

In general, being unreasonable can cause a fair amount of pain, and unreasonable requests definitely cause pain. They cause opportunity loss, which is painful. They cause sacrifice, which is painful. For many people, staying focused is painful, and giving up some of their playful distractions is painful. For others, the very idea of making a commitment or a decision is painful, and certainly stepping outside of a comfort zone—the very core of unreasonableness—is painful.

But organizations that are committed to getting extraordinary results get used to it. Pain is just what happens when your system experiences something different from what it has gotten used to, and as a result, the nervous system thinks that something is wrong. Pain is a given.

When you step outside your comfort zone and all your training and experience is screaming, "I don't belong here, outside the norms," that's when you feel pain. Or when you're making a commitment to something about which you're not sure, you're experiencing discomfort and dislocation, and your brain calls that pain. Talk to people who have gone through a merger; they'll all tell you it's painful. Has anyone been physically traumatized? No, they just feel dislocated. Pain. Many people even say that being promoted was painful. Why? Same reason.

Each time you or your organization (perhaps we should say your organism) feels the pain of being unreasonable, examine whether or not something is actually wrong. Once you are sure that while things are new or different, they are not wrong, the pain will subside. But pain is different from suffering. Suffering happens when people choose to continue feeling pain.

Suffering is the pain of feeling pain. Once we've decided that something is, in fact, wrong, we tend to make it worse. Our typical response includes wallowing, moaning about how bad things are, looking for fellow sufferers to commiserate with, crying "Why me?" and engaging in all sorts of other self-indulgent behavior intended to announce our pain to the world. That's suffering.

It's tough to choose not to have pain, especially if you're out in the world attempting something bold. But you can choose not to suffer; it's just another act of the will. Whenever you feel the pain, rather than defaulting to wallow mode, pay attention to what is really happening. Sometimes just paying attention to the pain and asking what is causing it is enough to make the pain subside. More often, you'll have to shift your attention somewhere else, perhaps willing yourself to focus on the intended outcomes. That will usually work, and it works on many levels: the physical, mental, spiritual, and even the corporate level.

Pain is not bad. It's an indication that something has happened that is different from what you expected, and pain is the call to find out if everything is all right. Sometimes pain means something bad and can be the result of one of our unreasonable actions having gone wrong. If there's really something wrong, go fix it. Otherwise, take the unreasonable approach and say, "This is different, but it's OK." Make sure everything really is OK, and move on.

Reasonable people shy away from unreasonable things because they intuitively understand the pain these things will cause. They prefer the tried, true, safe, and comfortable because they don't want to upset anyone or ruffle any feathers. They are polite, reserved, and measured because they know that this is how they're expected to behave. No one likes to be asked for commitments and promises, and most people would like their little worlds left intact. Being unreasonable challenges everything that is expected by your team, your peers, your customers, your vendors, your bankers, even your press—everyone expects you to play within the bounds of normal experience, and people get offended, and, yes, even pained if you transgress.

So it's particularly good news to know that the pain of being unreasonable, while inevitable, can be short-lived. Just train the people around you to get used to it. They also have to learn that the suffering is optional.

It is said that on the other side of pain is joy. Unreasonable strategies and tactics, properly applied, have the potential to reward your company with unheralded success, and the credit for that success should be shared.

Reward the Successful

If you're going to unreasonably ask people to go above and beyond, to work hard and stretch themselves—all on your behalf—you have to give them something in return. High-performing people expect to be rewarded for their efforts. If you want them to consistently produce extraordinary results, you have to ante up. There are four main categories of reward: financial rewards, nonfinancial incentives, public acknowledgment, and general celebration. As you can see, only one of them is going to actually cost you money.

Financial rewards are almost self-explanatory. Bonuses and other monetary incentives can be proper rewards for a heroic effort. They don't have to be large, but they do have to be significant relative to the recipient's regular compensation. Also, stay away from salary raises, or any other form of reward that becomes permanent.

There are two schools of thought on whether to preannounce bonuses, and they are both valid. The first is that you should preannounce a job-well-done bonus because it acts as an incentive to drive your team forward. The other theory is that if you preannounce, then you take away the element of discretion. Saving the announcement for last allows you to decide who, when, and how much, and the delay can genuinely delight your team.

Tom Matzen, CEO of Parmasters Golf Training Centers, insists that nonfinancial rewards have a much greater impact than mere money. He backs this up by saying that when you give people money, it just gets thrown in with all their other money, and it often gets spent without anyone noticing. On the other hand, a nonfinancial reward—it could be a weekend getaway trip for two, a new home theater system, some golf lessons, or even an evening out at an upscale local restaurant—is an experience that engages the beneficiary. People are much more likely to remember that it happened and to associate all the good feelings they have about it with you. This is especially true if you do give them something like a paid vacation, where their memories will always be tied to you, or a home theater, when they will think of you every time they watch. Reasonably, all people want more money. You, however, want them to remember that they did something extraordinary, and that they were rewarded for it, and for this the nonmoney rewards work best.

Public acknowledgment is a great way to compensate people for their unreasonable efforts. This can be something as toned-down as an e-mail broadcast to your team or singling someone out at a staff meeting. You can put the hero's name in a printed newsletter that goes to all your stakeholders. Don't be afraid to lavish praise and attention. Generally, the more the better—be effusive, be gushy. Don't worry about embarrassing them, but do be sincere.

And don't forget celebrations for your significant successes. Celebrations can range from lunchtime pizza parties to deluxe affairs at a local hotel, dinner and dancing cruises, or even balloon rides with champagne. Go public and tell your people what a great job they've done. Never treat their efforts as normal behavior or as if they were something you expected (even if you did just that). Loudly proclaim your people's extraordinary effort, and thank them profusely. Tell them there'll be more where that came from. Of course, you can combine public acknowledgment and even gift giving with any of your celebrations.

Once you've made the choice to drive, instead of say, fly or take the train, you have to put the car in gear, apply foot pressure to the gas, turn the wheel to steer, and judiciously apply the brakes. You'll never get anywhere unless you're willing to keep that up until you reach your goal. That's execution.

CHAPTER 6

UNREASONABLE
EXECUTION

Strategy gets you on the playing field, but execution pays the bills.

—Gordon Eubanks, CEO, Symantec, Inc.

82% of Fortune 500 CEO's surveyed indicated that they feel their organization did an effective job of strategic planning. Only 14% of the same CEO's indicated that their organization did an effective job of implementing the strategy.

—*Forbes* magazine

A survey done in 2005 by *The Economist* stated that "if companies were to become highly skilled at execution and realize the full potential of their current strategies, the increase in performance would be nearly 60%, on average. . . . If [they] were to become 'very effective' at execution, they would expect operating profits to improve by an average of 30% for each of two years, respondents said."

Companies need to learn how to execute.

Strategy, design, planning, and tactical selection are all critical parts of your business, and each increases your leverage dramatically. By positioning your resources in the best possible way and selecting the most effective tactics at your disposal, you increase your chances of success so that when you actually get going, you will be much more effective with plan A than with plan B or plan C. But all the thinking, strategizing, and planning in the world will not produce one lick of results—nada—without your actually *doing it*. You have to put it into effect—in fact, that's the very definition of the word *execution*.

There are some problems with the very issue of execution, the first of which is that execution is not the glory job. Witness the five Ps of the U.S. Navy rule: *Prior Planning Prevents Piss-poor Performance*. None of those five P's has anything to do with execution. The military strategists get the medals, not the grunts on the front lines. And no one volunteers to be an "execution specialist." Bill Johnson, CEO of H. J. Heinz, sums it up perfectly:

> No MBA wants to learn about execution. It's not exciting. Strategy is exciting. Thinking about The Big Thing is exciting. But execution is far more important.

Johnson knows what he's talking about. Heinz is a 100-year-old company, and you'd imagine that by now the growth has been all wrung out. In fact, the company had more revenue growth in the past year than in the five before. Johnson believes that in a mature market like his, where there are no surprises left, the company owes the entire increase to hard-driving sales execution.

Why Is Strategic Execution So Hard?

> *"The elements of the Dell business model are no secret . . . so why haven't other companies been able to copy your model?" "Because it takes more than strategy. It takes years of consistent execution for a company to achieve a sustainable competitive advantage."*
>
> —Michael Dell, in *Harvard Business Review*

With all we know about the crucial payoffs of executing your company's strategies reliably, why is it so hard for executives and entrepreneurs to master this? Why don't companies spend more time and resources perfecting processes that get things done? Why can't more companies build *this* into their DNA?

First, managers (if they get trained for anything) get trained to plan, not to execute. When I went to business school, the MBA catalog had dozens of courses devoted to strategy: marketing strategy, competitive strategy, corporate strategy, financial strategy, product strategy, even hiring strategy. Now, I believe in strategy, but it may be a case of too much of a good thing, because today's MBA curricula typically have not one single course devoted to the execution of those strategies.

Think about the wild success of books such as David Allen's *Getting Things Done* and the perennial bestseller, Neil Fiore's *The Now Habit*. While neither of these books is really about execution, the titles do promise some insight. Larry Bossidy and Ram Charan's blockbuster *Execution* takes aim squarely at this problem and owes much of its success to its brilliant title. No one is trained in execution, and most business owners don't have the faintest idea of how to get people to act consistently.

Second, executives and entrepreneurs alike often believe that the hands-on doing is most profitably left to the rank and file. When executives consider the value of their time or of their ability to contribute a certain unique skill set, it can easily seem as if *getting things done* is grunt work. I know a number of entrepreneurs who credit their success to completely removing themselves from the *doing* loop. In the end, the top management tiers of companies large and small not only don't focus on execution, they turn completely away from it. After all, top managers reason, once the hard planning work is out of the way, following the plan should be easy. Leaders believe that if they are clear about telling people to do the right thing, it will get done. Of course, we all know in our hearts that nothing could be farther from the truth.

The third, and possibly the biggest, barrier standing in the way of successful execution is the mistaken belief that strategy and execution can somehow be separated. We know from Field Marshall von Moltke's dictum about battle plans that strategies don't survive very long in their initial form, but must be adjusted and adapted continuously during the ensuing battle. The same holds true in the commercial arena. Strategies and plans are pristine in the early stages of a campaign, but as soon as you come belly to belly with competitors and customers, there is the need for constant tweaking, tuning, readjustment, and rearrangement. When strategy and execution are held apart as separate functions in the care of different individuals, strategies become fixed for the duration, and execution is going to suffer.

Not only are the responsibilities for execution kept separate, but isolating strategy from execution also has the effect of *excluding* the executers from the strategy process, which often results in strategies that can't really be executed. These strategies are created in an atmosphere charged with "wouldn't it be great if" without regard to whether the organization is capable of carrying them out. These strategies are not unreasonable; they are impossible.

Perhaps the last difficulty of execution is that execution involves a lot of people and takes place over an undefined and relatively long period of time. Strategy is typically formulated by a limited number of individuals over a limited and somewhat short period of time. Execution involves almost the entire organization, potentially scores or hundreds of people with conflicting agendas and game plans, and occurs over months and sometimes years. This long time frame makes it hard for normal players to stay focused and concentrate their efforts.

Crises arise, new organizational challenges pop up, the marketplace shifts, tastes change, and competitors do nasty, unpleasant things. This chaotic drift coupled with the natural tendency to get bored and turn toward other issues makes execution of strategy very difficult. Unreasonable strategy and planning position your company for breakthroughs, but the breakthroughs won't happen without disciplined execution. That is why we say that when you come right down to it, "execution is the only thing."

Over the long haul, successful strategy execution requires many of the attributes covered elsewhere in this book. First and foremost is the development of a culture of discipline and will. Corporate willpower is necessary to go the distance—to begin to execute on a plan and to continue relentlessly in the face of the chaos and turbulence in the market. Successful execution begins with the highest-level corporate commitment to launching a campaign, along with a priori agreements of continued management support. Aggressive execution also requires willpower at the "doer" level, the will to remain constant to the programs at hand. And because nothing in the world is ever as easy as it looks, unreasonable requests must become the norm—execution always requires asking for more than the planners originally believed necessary. The entire execution team has to adapt to an unreasonably high level of function. A shift to something much greater than the average 90 minutes of daily productivity is necessary in companies that want to get anything big done.

Unreasonable accountability—developing the kind of organization where people make commitments and are expected to honor them—is another key to fruitful execution programs. The standard in business is to let people off the hook for things they have not accomplished. "Be reasonable," people say. *No, don't be reasonable*—not if your goal is delivering on the company's strategic goals. Hidebound bureaucracies are known for tolerating low productivity; breakthrough companies bent on producing extraordinary results can't afford to do so.

The unreasonable execution formula is simple: *expect the best and inspect everything*. Demand a lot from people and reward them publicly for delivering. Strengthen the corporate and individual will and make everyone accountable for their results. It sounds easy; it isn't. But it works.

Can You Really Count on 'Em?

A promise has real power. In that moment the promise becomes who you are rather than something you said; and your relationship to the world shifts. You find yourself producing results that seem discontinuous and unpredictable from the point of view of the spectator.

—Werner Erhardt, founder of EST

The first step toward consistently successful execution is building a culture of accountability. Accountability has gotten a bad rap in today's business environment. In the public's mind, people like "Chainsaw" Al Dunlop have equated accountability with getting fired for not making your numbers. For many, accountability has become a code word for "I'm history if I don't deliver."

It is one of those words that causes a lot of confusion for people. It shouldn't, and it's really pretty simple. Accountability is about making a promise to do something, along with expecting that you will be held to deliver on that promise.

Being accountable means that *people can be counted on* to produce a specific outcome. And by now you'll realize that this is a primary condition for successful execution. You give your word. Your team gives its word. Clients give their word. Everyone agrees that they are going to play their part: do what they said they would, when they said they would, and with the performance conditions that they agreed to. Accountability, delivered, means that it will work. Imagine having an entire team of people you can depend on. Imagine having an entire company full of "go-to guys."

In ancient Rome, the engineers had a tradition of ultimate accountability. Legend has it that after the capstone was hoisted into place and an arch was complete, the supporting scaffolding was removed for the first time while the engineers would stand beneath the arch. They demonstrated, at grave risk to their lives, that their work was good and could be counted on. That's it. No more, no less. You don't want innocent bystanders, only full-fledged players completely engaged in the process of whatever it is you're committed to. This is what is meant by ownership. "The job is mine. I own it. I also own the results, and I'll see that they get done."

It also means that when things don't happen as planned, it doesn't get swept under the rug. No one tries to "sleaze out" or dodge the fact that the job didn't get done as planned. And if the job turns out wrong, as things occasionally do, the owners look for ways to fix it instead of not showing up for work that day. And if new promises are called for, they are made right then and there.

Accountability means "You can count on me to do what I said I'd do."

When each member of your team is willing to be held accountable, the work moves along more quickly because people's natural tendencies to say "I don't want to" or "I don't feel like it" are submerged into the general feeling that there is something greater at stake. All the socially acceptable things that tend to drag down performance, all the little things that fritter away productive time become unacceptable and frowned upon. It can get to the point where team members who aren't doing their part are shunned. *Peer pressure alone, constructively applied, will deliver dramatic execution gains.*

Another welcome phenomenon is the spontaneous formation of a "no whining zone." Previously it may have been OK to complain about the work, its difficulty, the conditions, the schedule—almost anything was reasonably fair game. In a culture of accountability, whining is not tolerated. The change is palpable, because as harmless as whining may seem, it drains people's energy and saps their will. Think about it: on the one hand, you are trying to master yourself, to will yourself to get something important done, and on the other, you get swept up in the complaint conversation happening in the next cubicle over. The self-imposed ban on whining brings welcome relief to all your serious players while exposing the ones who are not. Accountability is the secret sauce behind execution. With it, execution is actually a breeze. Without it, execution is almost impossible.

Sandy's company integrates equipment used in a public emergency system. The sales team had won its largest contract ever, but Sandy was concerned because the engineers had never, ever, in the company's 14-year history, delivered on time, and there were substantial penalties in the contract for being late. Engineers slipping their deadlines is nothing new. The general view is that the work is creative (strike one) and very complex (strike two) and that these types of employees are lone wolves who like doing it their own way and can't be held to a schedule (strike three). But this time, the accepted wisdom that generally condones being late would bring disaster for Sandy's company. She took an unreasonable, and unpopular, step and instituted a basic accountability program. The product development plan was reviewed by the entire technical team, all of whose members had to agree, first, that it was doable, that it was doable by them, and that it was doable on time. Next, the team posted the entire development schedule to an interactive Web site and managed deadlines and deliverables in real time. It held weekly all-hands staff meetings, the sole purpose of which was to discuss what was working, what was not working, and what else needed to be done to ensure success. The entire team agreed beforehand that it would keep to the schedule no matter what. This meant that any slippage would be caught up weekly with evenings and weekends. The team members never agreed to be ahead of schedule, but they agreed to stay on it. They kept this up for the entire project and delivered on time for the first time, to a very satisfied government client.

The Basic Accountability Tools in Execution

Consider the following list as a structure for accountability that will increase the reliability of any group project. Each element is necessary, and any missing element will create an opening for people to slip out of their commitments.

1. Unanimous agreement as to the desirability of the project and its alignment with the overall organizational goals
2. Agreement by each team member as to the doability of a project as defined, and, importantly, that they can and will do their parts
3. A mechanism for tracking tasks and their performance, as well as tracking specific deliverables and milestones to be met
4. A plan for catching up lost time on a short-term basis
5. Regular meetings to keep everyone on track and sort out little problems before they become big problems

6. A robust interteam communication system that allows ideas to flow freely and publicly

7. The willpower to hold all team members to their word

All of this may seem a little unreasonable; it's definitely not the way that most companies behave. Embracing this kind of commitment is transformational and will change the very nature of your company's relationship to producing big results.

Execution Is for Later

This may seem like a contradiction of the previous section; it is not, so bear with me. Take a look at tool number 5 in the preceding list. A key aspect of building high-accountability projects is to hold all-hands meetings that keep everything on track. These meetings typically revolve around solving small problems before they become big ones and dealing with bigger issues as they arise. Accountability meetings are critical for ensuring that your execution flows. It's so easy for people and teams to get off track just a little bit because of some glitch that no one can address. Those little bits start to pile up, one on top of the other, and become big bits in a short period of time. And it's not just one team, it's every team, and before you know it the whole company is heading for a train wreck. And it started so innocently . . .

Accountability meetings ensure that both small and large problems are dealt with swiftly. However, most corporate problem-solving meetings tend to follow predictable paths. Everyone means well, but most of the proposed solutions are based on some historical approach to solving the problem—using the methods that people "know" work. Remember what Peter Block said. People have a drive toward safety and security, and that includes making recommendations that are guided by what has worked well in the past, at least back then. But if those methods still worked, people would have already used them, right? For some reason, people never see this at the moment they are speaking.

They want to jump right back into execution, so they propose any solution they can think of just to be back in the game. To be effective in problem-solving meetings, you have to separate idea creation from execution. In other words, *execution is for later.* If you bring execution into the equation too early, you'll continue to formulate ineffective variations on what you've already tried.

The human mind is good at doing many different things well, but it is not so good at doing different things well at the same time. One way to improve the quality of your ideas is to separate generating ideas from evaluating ideas from executing ideas. Our reasonable tendency is to do these all at once, and this just doesn't work very well. Have you ever tried to make a list of ideas, and after about item four or five, you put down your legal pad, jumped up out of your chair, and started working on item one? The same thing happens in groups. Resist it—execution is for later.

Holding an unreasonable problem-solving meeting means keeping each of the stages separate. Of course, you won't have any problem keeping people zeroed in on evaluating an idea or developing an execution plan. The tricky part is maintaining the focus on creating new ideas. This is hard because it requires *thinking* and *focus*, two things that people are generally bad at.

Thinking Things

You've already read the chapter on unreasonable thinking, so you're prepared to learn how to think things that drive execution.

There seem to be two broad categories of thinking. One consists of free-form activities such as daydreaming and meditating, while the other is the disciplined process of asking questions and answering them. This is not the reasoned, rational cognitive science way of looking at it. No, not at all. This is unreasonable thinking: pragmatic, practical, and prescriptive.

Start by establishing a frame of mind that I call Green Light Thinking. Green Light Thinking essentially tells the brain that every idea is a go. Once the idea is explained, it requires no further validation. It goes on the list, without judgment, and you can move on to the next idea. Don't fall in love with any of your ideas at this stage, don't try to disprove them, and don't try to figure out the implementation. Just keep going until you have all the ideas you want.

That's all there is to it: ask the right questions and wait for the answers. How many? Establish a goal for new ideas. It might be 5, or it might be 50. Just as long as you come up with that many. If it's 50, don't be concerned that you come up with 50 good ideas. Trust the process: given all those ideas, when you start to sort them out, at least one of them will work.

Coming Up with All Those Ideas

The first way to come up with answers—or ideas—is basic brain-storming. Set a goal for the number of ideas, and Green Light everything. Appoint two people with neat handwriting to be your recorders. One writer captures one idea, and the other writer captures the next one so that you don't have to slow down for writing, which helps keep the ideas flowing. Also, audio record the entire meeting. Invest in the right technology to get conference table microphones and a recording device that can record 20 hours without stopping. Transcribe the recordings afterward to make sure that nothing was missed. You'll also like the record of all the subtleties and nuances of the conversation, which can be quite valuable to help clarify an idea later.

Keep your recording gear set up for all your meetings so that you can capture even casual get-togethers at the touch of a button. That way the best ideas don't get lost.

Use an unreasonable technique called Question Building. Gather your team. The group shouldn't be too large, no more than 15. Establish the context—the largest question on the table that you wish to think about. This could be something like "How do we fix this and such problem?" Based on the context, ask your team to generate a list of questions, the answers to which could lead to a solution to the problem. Keep this whole process

Green Light. Don't evaluate the second-level questions. You can either have people shout out what's on their minds or go around the room in order asking for questions. Next, switch gears to edit the questions so that they make sense, as not all of them will. Once you have the edited questions and have a nice, neat list, ask each question in turn. Have your group Green Light brainstorm on each of the questions.

Or you can try this unreasonable approach to brainstorming that I've used to produce some very interesting results. As before, start with your core question, usually how to fix something that's off course. Now select any handy book of wisdom. This could be the Tao Te Ching, the New Testament, the Torah, the Upanishads, Emerson's "Self-Reliance," or any other writing whose words you consider wise. Ask your question and then read a randomly selected passage. Try to relate the passage to your question. Let the passage help you generate some thinking. You'll be surprised at what comes out of people's mouths.

Try the following list of general questions and apply them to any thorny problem you have that is begging for a solution. Use the questions alone or in any combination with the thinking processes just discussed.

---

20 Unreasonable Questions You Probably Can't Answer Without Thinking Hard about Them

1. What would really open things to solve this problem?
2. What do you believe about the situation causing this problem?
3. How are these beliefs about this problem useful?
4. What are the issues that are causing this problem?
5. What are the processes that are critical to these issues?
6. What could be a breakthrough regarding these issues?
7. What part that's already working should we change?
8. What old stories or interpretations keep these issues in place?
9. If you only knew how to do it, what would you do?
10. If your resources were limitless, what would you begin immediately?
11. What about what we're saying isn't really true?

12. What wild solution would pay off so big that you would bet your future on it?
13. What would you need to know to be comfortable with this problem?
14. What impossible thing are you not committed to just because you think it's impossible?
15. If you weren't doing what you are doing, how would you solve this problem?
16. What part of this problem have you thought about before but never attempted to answer?
17. What kind of solution to this problem of yours inspires you?
18. What ideas about this problem frighten you because of their implications?
19. What things do you think you should stop doing immediately?
20. Is the solution to this problem animal, mineral, or vegetable?

The Art of Unreasonable Requests

Your number one task is to create an exciting, profitable vision for your company. Your number two task, just as important, is execution. If you're not the one getting your hands dirty, you're going to have to ask other people to take action. Employees, contractors, vendors, outsourcing partners—it makes no difference; you're still going to have to make requests for action. In fact, making requests is a key aspect of your day job, so you'd better get good at asking people to do things *so that those things get done*. Sounds simple, right? Far from it.

All action in the world begins with someone asking for something. Linguist John Searle made this clear in his book *Speech Acts*. He calls it "making requests," and says it this way:

> A request expresses a desire for the addressee to do a certain thing and normally aims for the addressee to intend to and, indeed, actually do that thing. A promise expresses the speaker's firm intention to do something, together with the belief that by his utterance he is obligated to do it, and normally aims further for the addressee to expect, and to feel entitled to expect, the speaker to do it.

Sure, Searle's wording is a little obscure, but follow his logic. Does anyone do anything meaningful without someone asking him to, and without him promising to do so? (Perhaps in the case of the self-motivated, but then it is you making requests of yourself and then agreeing to them.) Making requests causes the people in your company to carry on the business of the company. Want something done? Just ask. And if you're the senior executive or the owner, people say yes, and that thing gets done. That's called power. But requests carry their own little problem.

Most of us, even leaders, hate rejection. So we ask for small things, easy-to-do things, wimpy things. It is rare that we ask for what we really hope someone will be able to accomplish—or even agree to. We cut back our expectations. Our scaled-down requests make it easy for others to say yes, but those requests also bring us results far below what we really want. After a while, we just accept the fact that we can't ask too much from people, and our expectations drop without our realizing it.

Here's a secret that can make this easier for you. Linguistically, a request is different from an order or a demand. Someone (Searle's "addressee") doesn't have to say "Yes, sir." She can say no to your request. She can counterpropose offering a different solution. Even if you are the big boss, your people can say "No, it can't be done," or "No, I can't do it—at least, not now," or something like that. All promises are voluntary, and free will is involved. The other party can evaluate the possibility of whatever it is you asked, and then decide.

Now, of course, people may think what you're asking is wildly "unreasonable" but decide to say yes anyway. That's their call. But once they do, it's your job to support them to succeed. Don't approach this frivolously.

"Ask, and it shall be given you; . . . knock, and it shall be opened unto you," says the New Testament. If you're going to knock, don't be meek about it, no matter what it says about "the meek shall inherit the earth." They weren't talking about being unreasonable. Why ask for things that are reasonable and easy to deliver?

Knock on the big doors. Knock loudly.

This is not only about making requests of employees, but of partners, contractors, vendors, customers, lenders, investors—anyone with whom you interact and in whom you need to cause action. It also extends to favors. If you're going to owe someone for a favor anyway, make it in exchange for a huge favor. Make it a favor that someone would be happy to have you owe them. Be unreasonable; ask for the whole enchilada.

Back to John Searle for a moment. Nothing happens until you ask someone for something. And you already know that big strategies, the kind that come from unreasonable strategies of possibility, require big action. And nothing big happens unless you ask for something big. This means that if you've committed your company to any significant course of action, your small requests cannot get the job done. You've got to ask people for a lot. The only way to make big things happen is to up the ante and make your requests unreasonable requests.

Unreasonable Requests Motivate

Besides increasing productivity, big requests are motivating. After all, would you rather do something significant, even glorious, or would you prefer some small task, the results of which no one will ever hear about? If there's anyone on your team who says the small task, fire that person immediately.

That doesn't mean people won't approach your challenge with fear and trembling. We talked before about courage, and courage isn't doing something dangerous; rather, it is acting in the face of fear. A bit of courage may be needed if you're asking something unreasonable, but along with that comes a feeling of heroism. People want to feel as if what they're doing is meaningful, daring. They may even be called upon to rescue the company. They are doubly motivated by the notion that what you've asked is life or death.

My first business partner, Bruno Henry, often told our troops that the company was in dire straits (which it was) and that saving it—along with saving their own jobs—would require an act of huge commitment on their parts. Occasionally he exaggerated the depths of financial despair, but he always praised our employees' valor and called forth their willingness to help rescue our business. Even though this drama went on for three years, they never tired of hearing about it, and they never failed to rise to the challenge.

More Cycles and Bigger Bites

If you reduce your cycle time—the time it takes to get something done—you can accomplish more cycles. In the same way, within any given cycle, and with any given resource, if you accomplish more by asking for more, your productivity will skyrocket.

One of my colleagues told me about a sales job he took when he was in his early twenties. For each of his first three months, he grossed $125,000 for the company, which he thought was great. His boss, though, told him that was nothing. The person hired just before my colleague was bringing in $300,000 a month, and the firm's top producer was raking in over a million dollars a month. My colleague's boss said if he didn't triple his gross, he was out.

You or I, looking at the situation from the outside, might have thought that the boss acted unfairly. After all, didn't the company share in my colleague's sales responsibility? Shouldn't his boss have told him at the outset what kind of sales figure was acceptable? Shouldn't the boss have offered him some guidance and resources, which would have helped shore up sales?

Those are reasonable questions, but that's not the situation my colleague was in. An unreasonable request had been made of him: "Triple your sales or you're out." He didn't debate its fairness. He had to pay his rent. In his mind, he declared a state of emergency. He started taking action, fast. Instead of his usual 15 prospecting calls a day, he started making 30, 40, even 50 calls a day. He also bought sales technique books and read them each night. The next day, he'd try out at least one new technique. If it worked, he'd keep it in his arsenal. If it didn't, it was on to a new one. The following month, he made the company its $300,000 and kept his job. The funny thing is that his monthly figures continued to rise after that. After a year, he was one of the firm's top producers.

He told me that in the beginning, when he brought in $100,000, he thought he was doing all that he could do. But after getting the ultimatum, he saw that he'd been dragging his feet without realizing it. His boss's request woke him from the limits of his reasonable behavior and expectations.

Unreasonable requests, of course, don't always have to be so confrontational. One of my clients made an unreasonable request in the form of a special sales offer that saved his technology company. His firm was having a slow period and was dangerously short on cash. If it had gone more than a couple of months without a substantial payday, it would have folded. Fortunately, it won a seven-figure contract. Still, there was a problem.

The standard for the industry was payment in thirds. The customer would pay a third up front, a third after it tested the software, and a third when it signed off on the finished product. For my client, payment terms like that wouldn't work. To keep his doors open, he needed the entire payment right away. It was time for an unreasonable request—something totally unexpected in his industry.

He presented his customer with a startling offer. Along with the software, he'd give the customer at-cost training services and a full money-back guarantee. All he asked for was full payment up front. He wanted every penny before his company even drew up the design. His customer was stunned. The at-cost training and guarantee were outrageous enough. But the request that it pay several million dollars without knowing if the product would do its job was unheard of. The customer sat on the offer a few days but eventually agreed. My client was saved.

What would an unreasonable request look like for you?

If you normally pay $50,000 for a piece of machinery, ask your supplier to sell it to you for $25,000.

If it normally takes your company six months to roll out a
new product, ask that people do it in two.

If you normally ask your staff for a 3 percent sales increase,
ask for an increase of 100 percent.

Big Requests Cost No More Than Small Ones

It should be clear to you that you're going to have to ask for
something if you want anything to happen. If you don't formally
make requests, you turn your entire business into a haphazard
affair where people do what they choose on their own schedules
(which perfectly describes some businesses I've seen).

Since you're going to ask, however, you may as well make your
asking big. Since you are making requests, your people can say
no just as easily. Large requests—just like large favors—cost you
no more than small ones.

Ask people to do things you think you have no right to expect
from them. Ask them to do things to which you think they'll
say no. But ask anyway. Here's the trick: expect them to say yes
and don't worry about whether they do or they don't. If all the
people on your team were continually unreasonable in their
requests of one another and, at the same time, fully, confidently
expected that their requests would be met, what would happen?
What if you made it a game, the object of which was to promise
to deliver no matter what—do you think that would rocket your
project or your business forward? *Of course it would.*

Just as making formal requests is not a normal activity for most
people in businesses, unreasonable requests are doubly abnormal.
Making an unreasonable request takes guts. You'll shock some
people. Others may get angry. If what you want to accomplish is
important enough, though, temporarily shaking up some people
won't matter much. If you have fully embodied the result you
want to produce, then you'll make the kinds of requests that will
create that result.

Whatever you were going to ask for, ask for more. Whenever you wanted it, ask for it sooner. Whatever you were willing to pay or trade, ask for it for free—or as a gift. You get the idea. Your business will move forward in direct proportion to the size of the requests, so to move things along quickly, you have to ask big. You have to ask unreasonably. Make your requests big. Ask for more. Ask for it quicker. Ask for it cheaper. Take anything you were going to ask for and amplify it.

You might want to start now. Get out a ruled pad, draw a line down the middle, and number the rows from 1 to 10. In the left column, write, "Reasonable Requests I Was Going to Make," and in the right column, write, "Those Requests Made Unreasonable." Now, simply fill in the blank lines. For example, your reasonable request might be, "Bill, I need this by Friday." Your unreasonable revision might be, "Bill, I need this tomorrow morning." Or you may be planning on calling your banker, Yvonne, and asking for a 30-day extension on a loan. Your unreasonable request could be, "Yvonne, I need to increase my line of credit 50 percent, and I need to extend the terms." You get the idea. Do the unreasonable: Ask for a lot. You may get it.

Unreasonable requests also come in the form of asking people to do things that are just not done "that way." Someone who consistently asks people to do things differently, perhaps unreasonably, is Ralph Whitworth, founder of Relational Investors.

In 1999, Whitworth was called in to serve as chairman of the board of Waste Management, Inc., to help stabilize the company after a disastrous plunge in share prices. "Both shoes had already dropped," and it appeared as if stability was ahead. But within a week of taking over, the share price dropped again. As was common at that time in the case of big share-price drops, a lawsuit began against the company's management. However the case ultimately wound up, it could stretch on for a long time, and while it was pending—it could take years to reach a jury—there would be a dark cloud hanging over the company's stock. Whitworth knew something unreasonable was called for, and he decided to settle the case. Even more unreasonably, he decided to settle it in the quickest and most expeditious way possible—he decided to settle it himself.

He called a meeting with Denise Nappier, treasurer of the State of Connecticut, which was the lead plaintiff and acting as surrogate for everyone in the class action suit. Lawyers for both sides insisted that they couldn't settle, that it simply wasn't possible because they had not been through the discovery process; without reading the thousands of pages of documents and testimony, there was no way to honestly assess the value of a settlement.

Part of the reason for the length of the discovery process is that attorneys have to justify their need for looking at each document, as both sides try to protect privileged and possibly damaging information from getting into the other side's hands. This gave Whitworth his idea.

Now this is where unreasonable execution—coming up with an approach that goes far beyond normal people's thinking—can really pay off. Whitworth suggested that the Waste Management team gather every last document that could in any way be related to the case and put them all in one big room for 90 days. Attorneys for either side could come and go as often as they liked, for as long as they liked, they just couldn't leave the room with any of the material.

The security lawyers said Whitworth was "whacko," that his plan was impulsive and dangerous. Whitworth simply thought it was the best way to get his company back in action. Nappier agreed to the plan.

In record time—four months—the two sides reached an agreement, with Waste Management paying the second largest settlement then known in securities law. It totaled $500,000,000, or about $1 per share, a huge sum at the time; but because the cloud—the uncertainty—was lifted, the share price started up, rising $2.50 a share within days. Everyone else was looking at the cost, while Whitworth had already calculated the cost/benefit.

Following this coup, Whitworth withdrew all guidance—a company's public estimates of it's future profit potential. He told the Wall Street investment analysts, "You can't rely on anything we've said in the past, and we're going to reconstruct our statements for the whole company."

This is something that just isn't done very often. You can imagine the Herculean task this could be for a company as large as Waste Management. The auditors, Arthur Andersen, said it was "impossible." But Whitworth said that not only was he going to do it, he had to—that it was the only way to restore investor confidence in the company. This had to happen, and it had to happen fast. He gave the financial team an unreasonable 10 weeks (10 weeks!) to reanalyze 600 profit centers. The team set up a war room (a fairly common idea with unreasonable thinkers) and hired 2,000 hand-picked temporary auditors. Working from 5 p.m. until exhaustion each night, the temporary audit army along with the permanent staff went over the books until the project was complete. In the end it took 16 weeks, and ultimately, the company wrote off $1.7 billion in assets, crafting a pristine set of financial statements that have never needed another write down or significant adjustment.

Beware the Voice of Reason

> *When either the political or the scientific discourse announces itself*
> *as the voice of reason, it is playing God, and should be spanked and*
> *stood in the corner.*
>
> —Ursula K. Le Guin, commencement address,
> Bryn Mawr, 1986

Perhaps the biggest block standing in the way of being unreasonable is the voice of reason. That is the dialogue that either pops up in your head or comes from someone else's mouth that says something like, "Be reasonable. It's just not done that way."

You listen to this paean to logic and normalcy, and it is easy to be seduced into thinking, "That's right. That *would* be wrong."

Stop right there.

What we call reasonable has developed over time—years, decades, centuries—as a measured response that is low in risk and low in effort. While that response was probably a good thing when it began, given its nature and long history, it is now likely to produce only average results. Why? Because all the highs and lows have been edited out through the passage of time and many executions—what statisticians call "trials."

The lows are filtered out by risk avoidance and general sloth; that's what gets "reasonable" started in the first place. People try to avoid risk and minimize their efforts, and over time, approaches that satisfy these criteria become normal. But playing it safe is not sufficient for a thing to become normal—it also has to have a positive attraction. So things that combine a low perceived risk, limited exertion, and high reward are very attractive. But the highs, or great results, get filtered out by a process called regression to the mean.

Think of it as an above-average return on investment. Low cash in, high reward out. We know from economics that the price of great investments rises over time as more and more people seek the (relatively) high rewards. Pretty soon, it's high cash in for high reward, and the relatively high reward is now just average. It's the same thing with reasonable. What started out as modest effort for high reward is no longer that. Over time, by continuous application of the tried and true, whatever exceptional results that once were achieved no longer are. On top of that, the same level of effort has to increase just to produce poorer and poorer results.

At the end of the day, normal, or reasonable, equates to mediocre.

Reasonable evolved to stay within the bounds, to never offend anyone, to push no one's buttons, to strain no systems, and to keep everyone well within her comfort zone. So whenever you hear the voice of reason whispering in your ear, you must ask yourself, do you want to create extraordinary results or not? As you can see, being reasonable has being ordinary built right in.

Being reasonable has no choice but to yield right around the aver-age. Moderate. Fair to middling. So-so. Run of the mill. Typical. Tame. Gentle. Measured. Reasonable people find all these accept-able, especially since the goal is to keep things on an even keel, avoid risk, and not work too hard.

If it's extraordinary results that you seek, by definition, they cannot come from reasonable actions. Extraordinary results can come only from unreasonable actions. And unreasonable actions can come only from unreasonable requests.

Make sure your team is populated with people who want to take this ride with you. You'll find out soon enough who is and who isn't ready. *Good to Great* author Jim Collins says that one of the keys to business success is having the right people on the bus. Make sure your team members are going to be happy when the bus goes really fast and be certian they're willing to hop off and push when the bus breaks down.

Playing Both Sides

Reasonable people choose sides. They place bets and hope that they're right. But how often will that be? The odds say that for an uneducated bet, you'll be correct about half the time. And the more you know, the more information you have, the greater the odds are in your favor. But even then, you could be wrong a lot of the time—especially in businesses that rely on conditions that are beyond your control.

There's another approach that comes from Wall Street traders. Traders want to make money no matter what. External factors are often incompressible and unpredictable, and traders have no time for losing—if they lose too often, they are quickly out of a job. So they've developed techniques that are referred to as hedging, as in hedging your bets.

Option traders have one group of strategies called spreads. Basically, spread traders buy one commodity and sell another, or they buy and sell the same commodity in different markets or for different time frames. Depending on the exact spread type, spread traders can make money whether the thing they are buying goes up or down, and they can make money whether the market goes up or down.

A long straddle is a bet on high volatility. It makes money if the value of the underlying asset moves either up or down significantly. A short straddle is a bet on low volatility. It makes money as long as the value of the underlying asset does not change too much. Then there are more exotic-sounding strategies, such as strangles, collars, fences, and butterflies, and each one is designed to take advantage of a general sense of things rather than a specific outcome.

But here's the interesting part: traders can make money no matter which way the market moves—up, down, or sideways. While they may find it frustrating when the market doesn't move at all—there's no action and no big profits—smart traders can still make a profit by doing what is called *writing* the options, which means that even though there is no trading profit, they can capture the option premium.

Farmers play this game differently. If the price of corn goes up, then a corn grower can make a lot of money selling the crop. But what happens if the price goes down? Farmers address that possibility by using some of the same tools that Wall Street traders use—futures and options hedging. While they hope that prices will go up, they fundamentally place a bet that prices will go down. If prices do fall, they can make up some of the lost crop price with the increasing value of their hedge. Of course, there are costs to doing this; insuring against risk is not free. But it is something to think about. Many sophisticated farmers end up as futures traders and supplement their incomes thereby.

There are also other ways to play this game. A client of mine, David Drozd of Ag-Chieve, located in Winnipeg, Manitoba, advises farmers on how to best hedge the market with nonfinancial strategies. David started life as a grain farmer and, after 20 years of family farming, now advises farmers all across the Canadian prairies on whether he thinks crop prices will go up or down, and, more important, what to do about it and how to protect themselves without using futures or options. Grain farmers can lock in a profit and protect themselves against a drop in price, just as livestock producers can secure their feed requirements and protect themselves against an increase in price by hedging their requirements in the cash grain market.

Traditional execution takes a point of view and goes for it. But if your business depends largely on forces beyond your control, you have to acknowledge that and act accordingly. Successful execution requires realizing that sometimes things go your way, and sometimes they go the other way. The unreasonable approach requires seeing both sides and making hedge bets so that either way is your way.

Who Wins and Who Loses

VF Imagewear owns the rights to print National Football League logos on T-shirts, hats, and other clothing. One of VF's agreements allows it to sell a reproduction of championship teams' jerseys. But these are commodities with a very short shelf life; after all, the enthusiasm for this kind of product wanes pretty quickly after the big game, so VF must move fast. How does it do that?

It plays both sides, of course. Once the football playoffs are complete, it's got it narrowed down to the next level's teams. "It requires planning 19 weeks ahead of time to ship division champion, conference championship, and [shirts for] both teams in the Super Bowl," said Ed Doran, VF's president. "For every team that's left in the playoff hunt, you have to have the artwork done and make the film for every type of T-shirt for each of the teams." VF has its bases covered, farming out different teams to different printers, so that everybody is all set up and ready to go at a moment's notice. The company wins either way, as long as the game doesn't get canceled.

Don't bet on what's going to happen; position yourself to benefit from change. Look on both sides of the playing field—what can change in your business? What happens if things go one way? What if they go the other way? What would that mean to your business? How can you take advantage of movement on either side? Looking at both sides—that's the trick. And it requires that you loosen your preconceptions and lose your prejudices.

Jerk Leadership

Being unreasonable—making big requests, demanding account-ability, even asking your team members to think harder and exercise their brains—can put you way out on a limb. After all, you are *being unreasonable*, and you are violating some, if not all, of the norms that reasonable people have come to expect and accept. You're coming up with strange ideas, pushing people far beyond their comfort zone, and asking them for a lot.

This can easily get interpreted as you being a jerk.

"Jerk" is not a term commonly used in polite society. *Webster's* calls a jerk a "stupid or foolish" person, but the term usually means someone who doesn't know how to behave properly or, more to the point, someone who is behaving badly. Reasonable people often think that a boss who is *being unreasonable* is a *jerky boss*. It seems that if you go down this path, there may be no way to avoid jerkhood.

Being a jerk has two sides to it. Jerks needlessly irritate and anger those around them, and if you get a reputation for being one, people may stop listening to you. You want to avoid this aspect of jerkiness. On the other hand, being a jerk can have a positive aspect. Jerkhood is quite liberating; it gives you the freedom to ask for—not demand—whatever you want, knowing that your team's somewhat bad opinion of you is actually OK. It's important to state that you can pull off this second aspect only if you also have a reputation for creating great results.

You want to make sure you're not putting the cart before the horse. If you already have a reputation for bringing wins to your company, then you can get away with a lot of unreasonable-type behavior before people start hurling epithets your way. However, if that's not true, and you're taking up being unreasonable in an effort to deliver the goods, it may backfire on you. You may end up being a jerk.

Great business leaders who are called jerks are legion. Many of these leaders apply unreasonable strategies and tactics, and they survive jerkhood because they deliver the goods. The moral is, be unreasonable and make sure you succeed. Jerks who don't deliver end up creating cultures of despair and having severe turnover problems, leading to eventual business failure. Either way, embrace your jerkhood and ask that people give you their best. Make sure they win in the process, and win big. When they do, make sure they know that you know. Reward. Acknowledge. Celebrate. Make that happen and all the jerkiness goes away.

Don't Wait for Proof

When you're developing something new, be it a product or a service, it helps to make certain that there's a market for it, so you do the research, conduct studies, and run focus groups. Paraphrasing Mikhail Gorbachev from another context: trust, but verify. That's all smart and highly recommended, but there comes a point where you just have to trust your gut.

Especially if you're creating something genuinely new, you'll never have enough proof that it works. Why? Your prospects aren't really sure if they need your offering or not. Half the time, they aren't even sure what you're talking about. Look at fax machines. No one was screaming for them before they were invented. Putting documents in the mail seemed just fine, and actually people were partly right about that. Early adopters of fax machines had no one to fax to! Or consider the automatic teller machine, or ATM. The first focus groups for ATMs reacted in a violently negative way. They were sure that the machines would be unreliable and that bank employees would use machine failures as a cover for stealing money. And what's wrong with bank branches, anyway?

Testing brand new ideas is risky because people don't know and can't tell you how they will behave with respect to something they have never experienced. Plus, people tend to be skeptical of new ideas, and in some cases, like the ATM, can be downright hostile to them. Just like people inside companies, those outside don't want their ways of behaving changed under any circumstances, so new ideas can be unsettling, and if the ideas are new enough, they can be threatening. Most people simply don't have enough imagination to figure out how something new can be a benefit to them. Given a chance to vote, they will vote no.

Just as difficult is the case when you have developed a new business model—not a new product or service, but a new way of delivering or distributing it, or maybe a new pricing scheme, or a new means of production. Lots of these ideas can be worked out on paper, but until they are in full production, you really have no idea whether or not they will succeed.

It goes against the grain, but there are a lot of situations where you can do all the looking you want, but at some point, you still have to leap. You can't rely on market testing or any other form of proof, and there's no external way to develop certainty about your new idea. You just have to go with your gut and trust your intuition.

What is intuition, anyway? Is it some metaphysical, psychic, spiritual connection, or is there a more rational explanation? The real answer is that it may be a little of both. Most of what we call intuition is an amalgam of a large collection of data that we have absorbed at an other-than-conscious level, information that's been brewing and boiling in our brains. Don't think that these data get into your brain by accident—they're not a bunch of random thoughts brought together by chance. The unconscious part of your mind has been seeking out pieces of information—bits of conversation, things you read in the newspaper or hear on TV, products you pass by at trade shows or in showrooms or in retail stores, all selected by your reticular activation system as being somehow important to one of your many parallel streams of thought. And it's not like all these bits are thrown into a blender to concoct some new info cocktail. Rather, your unconscious mind is processing, selecting, sorting, rearranging, evolving, and filtering it all until somehow it makes sense.

When ready or when called upon, that "intuitive feeling" is our unconscious speaking to us; it's just often presented in a language that we have a hard time understanding, so it seems strange. It's not as if we hear voices in our heads commanding, "Do this. It will work." The intuitive communication is more subtle than that, more like, "Build it. They will come," which is why we have to trust our gut. Perhaps we simply need to have faith in that part of ourselves. Trusting your gut is a little like saying to yourself, "I think I understand; can you please tell me more," and accepting whatever it is you think is being said as true.

Yes, it is totally unreasonable. We've been raised to make our decisions based on observable, verifiable proof, not some internal voice that we can't clearly understand. However, once you realize that, especially for new ideas, the facts don't always speak for themselves, you may begin to trust that your internal processor, your intuition, may just have to do it for them.

Cut Your Timeline in Half

> *Big will not beat small anymore. It will be the fast beating the slow.*
>
> —Rupert Murdoch

When you're planning a project, it seems reasonable to build in slack. You want to make sure you can get it done no later than when you said, especially if you work in a culture that punishes failure. Not to contradict everything we've said about accountability and commitment, your goal is to execute and deliver the best results in the most effective, efficient, and productive way possible, and sometimes being later than you said is the cost.

Here's what happens. You want to make sure that you meet your deadlines, so you take your original timeline (which in itself was probably padded by whoever built the elemental steps) and add some slack to it. You call it insurance against emergencies. But by the time you've finished padding each step, building in the fudge factor, the result you're looking to achieve has receded weeks, or even months, into the future. This way you can't be late, and if you perform as well as you believe you will, you end up looking like a hero. Poker players and salespeople call it sandbagging, and it means holding back so that you appear stronger later on. In the world of corporate politics, holding back is probably a good idea. But if your goal is breakthroughs and extraordinary results, don't do this.

Don't argue with people's assessments of how long their parts will take. Accept all input, and build a game plan as you normally would. Do all the padding and bloating you want, then add one final step.

Cut your timelines in half.

When you halve all your timelines, everyone is put on red alert. The people involved will be forced to drop the padding and get to the result. What's more, the energy involved will bring about better work.

Use Parkinson's Law

C. Northcote Parkinson coined his famous law based on extensive experience in the bureaucratic British civil service. Parkinson noticed that as the British Empire declined in both size and importance, there was actually less work to be done. But the numbers of employees stayed level, and in some cases increased, and they were as busy as ever. He boiled these observations into Parkinson's Law:

Work expands to fill the time allotted to do it.

We don't need to explain Parkinson's Law; it is as true in business as gravity is on earth. All people at every level build slack into their work—and the slack will get used. And it's not just timelines that expand, but use of resources as well. Parkinson is also quoted as saying, "The demand upon a resource always expands to match the supply of the resource." Author Brian Tracy says it differently: "Expenses rise to meet income."

Because it's inevitable does not mean that it's necessary. When you cut your timelines and your resource requisitions, everyone will find a way to do more with less. People will be forced to work more efficiently. The ingenuity required will prompt stronger solutions. Creativity will jump through the roof.

Not only will things get done faster and cheaper, but they'll be better. Next, as they say in the shampoo business, rinse and repeat. Reduce your cycle time and double your number of cycles. If you are able to do the work in half the time, then double the number of cycles. Everything happens faster. A side benefit is that people tend to enjoy themselves more when they're engaged in vigorous action than when they're knee-deep in sloth. Apply this thinking to all forms of sandbagging. Accept your team's assertion that its time frames are valid, and then unreasonably ask the team members to reduce them.

Do It Right

It is in the rightness and the truth of the actions themselves that we gain the strength to do what needs to be done.

—Thomas Merton

Whenever you think of execution, there are the right ways and the wrong ways. The right ways are in accord with your vision and your values, and often lead to long-term profits and wealth. The wrong ways usually cut corners and sacrifice your principles, but they may have the benefit of bringing in short-term profits. The problems with doing it the wrong way are rife, but the biggest is that while short-term profits are the goal, doing it wrong doesn't always bring even those.

Despite what should be clear to everyone, doing it the wrong way, the expedient way, is pretty popular. People commonly explain away their principles and justify their methods in order to gain in the short term. The wrong way is often also the easy way. The quick way. The cheap way. Paradoxically, when viewed in this light, doing it the wrong way seems reasonable. Of course, you'd never call it "the wrong way," but that's what it is: wrong. Bad behavior has become not only acceptable, but institutionalized. Witness some of the recent spectacular corporate failures, such as Enron, WorldCom, Tyco, Global Crossing, and Barings Bank. However strong these companies may or may not have been, they were brought down by a culture of doing things the expedient way, the short-term way, the wrong way—at a cost of tens of billions of dollars in shareholder wealth.

Conversely, doing it right has become unreasonable. It is often slower and more expensive, with a longer path to rewards. "Do it the right way. Not the fast way, not the easy way. That's unreasonable." Tim Carter, Internet video guru and proprietor of AsktheBuilder.com, is an advocate of doing things the right way. Whether its in the context of repairing a leaky faucet, paving the driveway, or building a hugely successful business, Carter takes the approach that leads to long-term, stable results. What are the rewards? "Tremendous personal satisfaction coupled with great financial success. My income is 20 times what it was as a contractor, perhaps more."

Why does this work? Carter puts it this way. "Here's the payoff. Everything you or I buy—we are all consumers of something, whether it's food, tools, or gasoline, when you think about your user experience—how it works and how you have to work it—you want the product to do exactly what someone says it's going to do. And you want that both before and after the sale."

If you want consumers to be satisfied, you simply have to fulfill their expectations. In other words, do the right thing and give people what you promised them no matter how hard it is. When you do this, they will be not only satisfied but also loyal. A large percentage of Tim Carter's viewers and visitors are repeat customers because he makes clear promises telling people what they can expect, and then he fulfills those promises.

People take shortcuts to gain quick profits, winning the battle but often losing the war. Companies that take shortcuts are ones that people don't like and don't patronize twice. AskTheBuilder's competitors take the easy way out. They rarely tell the whole truth about a product, and they willingly lead readers down the garden path in order to advocate a product and reap commissions or referral fees. Carter talked about a press release he'd just received from a company selling corn furnaces that promise to heat your home on ears of dried corn. The price? A measly $5,000, which could be saved on heating in just one winter. Really? Most writers will just run the press release: the expedient thing. The wrong thing. But that's not the whole truth, and there are many unanswered questions. How is this going to work? How will the heat get distributed so that it can warm the whole house? Will the furnace need to be installed and integrated with your present system, and what will that cost? That would be the whole truth, and AskTheBuilder will ask those questions. This will surely cost the company product endorsement fees, but it will build consumer loyalty over the long haul. That's the hard way, but it's the right way. Unreasonably sticking to the unvarnished, unbiased truth has earned Carter and his AskTheBuilder brand a tremendous following. It may not be the fastest way to succeed, but doing things the right way will provide superior profits over the long haul. Unreasonably so.

Measure Everything

To execute to the highest level requires a baseline and a continual benchmark so that you can tell where you are at any moment. How else are you going to know which dial to turn or which knob to tweak?

Measure everything and keep tabs and performance statistics so that you can easily gauge whether a plan or program is working as expected. Some things are readily measured, such as revenue or head count or available capacity. Even the things that aren't directly measurable, such as customer satisfaction or market awareness, can be measured by proxy, and you can keep track of those.

Is it unreasonable to measure everything? No, it's one of the most rational things you can do. Measure, track, record, test. Keep deltas and standard deviations and figure out what's normal and what's acceptable. Then figure out whether you are getting closer to your goals or just treading water. It's amazing what gets revealed when you start keeping track. It makes the keep or ditch decision so much easier.

There's no way to make a list of all the things that an individual company should track, because each is so—well, individual, but here's how to find out. Make a list of all the critical elements in your business and devise a way to measure and track each one. Then make a list of all the critical change or enhancement programs you've got running and devise a way to measure and track those. Add measures to keep on top of your cash, your sales, your profits, your expenses, and all your other commitments, and you've got a solid control console with which to drive your company. This may sound a bit unreasonable—after all, how many measurements do you need? The answer is in the list you just made: you need as many gauges as you have important things happening in your company—nothing less will do. Unless, of course, you're willing to accept subpar performance.

After all, would you drive your car without knowing how fast you were going or how much gas you had in the tank? Probably not. And you'd also like to know whether your tires had air or not and approximately how much oil was in the crankcase, wouldn't you? But you're willing to drive your business, which is much, much more valuable, without information anywhere near as good.

Gaining control of this performance data will make your business nimble. It will enable you to see, at a glance, which parts of your business are working and which are not. And it will allow you to make tactical changes without feeling uncomfortable, because your decisions will be supported by a quick reading of your dashboard. Keep your eyes on your goal and measure your performance and progress by keeping your eyes on the dashboard. Make changes as they are necessary, as often as necessary, in order to squeeze the most possible performance from your business.

Measurement Motivates

In the military, they say, "What gets measured gets done." This may seem like something of a paradox, because in all things, people avoid accountability. Yet Frederick Taylor proved it a hundred years ago: just by measuring things, the things at least change. This happens at every level of an organization, from top to bottom. It's even true at the quantum level, the most fundamental layer of matter. In quantum physics, it has been proven that the very act of observing (or measuring) something causes that something to change. And in the world of strategies and tactics, this principle turns into a tool that you can use with great leverage.

Despite their protestations to the contrary, and the squiggling and squirming that goes on when you try to pin people down and get commitments, people have evolved to like and respond to clear goals. The clearer the better. The acronym SMART (specific, measurable, accountable, relevant, time-limited) was developed as a checklist for what makes a goal effective. Give someone a SMART goal, along with access to the necessary resources, and he is more likely to achieve it than if you simply tell him to do something vague or unspecified.

Moreover, goals not only help people succeed, but because they point so clearly to the path to success, they help people *feel* successful. So why does the average business executive avoid setting SMART goals if at all possible? What causes this paradox? The paradox stems from fear of failure. Reasonable people are afraid that they won't reach their goals, especially if these are aggressive goals that squeeze them out of their comfort zone. They know there is a risk that they won't make the deadline, or reach the measure, or whatever—and they view failure as, well, failure. And it's reasonable to avoid failure, isn't it?

No, it isn't. Avoiding failure—or even avoiding situations that you think are going to be hard to win, at least from the get-go—has one inescapable consequence, which is that you set weak, uninspiring, easy-to-achieve, low-growth targets for yourself and your business, and that leads to weak, uninspiring, low growth.

Unreasonable leaders set big goals—or as *Good to Great* author Jim Collins called them, *Big Hairy Audacious Goals*. They know that SMART audacious goals propel an organization forward, and that even when they don't reach them, companies with big goals have made more progress than they would have made without them. Remember the old chestnut, *"Reach for the stars and settle for the treetops."* And unreasonable leaders let their people know that falling short of a goal is not necessarily failure, as long as significant progress is made. Failure is making no progress at all. Failure is failing to act. The very act of measuring and putting SMART goals in place for each significant part of your business may seem unreasonable, but it might be the SMARTest thing you can do.

Efficiency versus Effectiveness

People are always trying to be efficient. Unreasonable people are trying to be both efficient and effective. What's the difference? Efficiency is getting things done more quickly, with a minimum of waste or expense and little or no unnecessary effort, while effectiveness is getting things done well. Effectiveness is getting the intended response from your actions. Both are important, and you shouldn't have to choose between them. But faster is not always better, and minimizing waste, as has been pointed out before, isn't our major focus. Unreasonable businesses are always striving to produce a particular outcome. They measure the results of their actions and seek to reach their goals by becoming more effective. Often, becoming more effective means abandoning one approach in favor of another that can get the job done not just faster, but better.

Effectiveness is paramount, and flexibility is key. Fixed ideas will crush the life out of your business as surely as your competitors and rapidly changing markets will if you're not willing to continually adapt. The tactics you choose are critical, but just as critical is your willingness to change tactics as soon as your control console indicators tell you to.

Remember von Moltke and his famous battle plan? It's not about putting a plan in place and seeing it through to the very end. That would be nice, but it isn't going to happen in this world. Things change. Pick your spots and leap into action.

This is even more true today than it was 150 years ago. In the twenty-first century, a business leader's primary job is to remain on high alert and to respond quickly to each new threat or circumstance. Annual planning is no longer enough, and your initial arrangement of resources and choice of tactics will never carry you to the end.

To manage uncertainty, you must be willing to scrap your carefully laid preparations at a moment's notice and make fresh decisions. While your company's strategic objectives may not vary much, your choice of tactics must remain fluid. You have to be completely unreasonable to succeed in today's environment of chaos and uncertainty.

Unreasonable leaders realize that they cannot eliminate uncertainty. They know that their strategies will not eliminate constant change, even confusion; their goal is to be prepared for the fact that all their preparations may fail and to manage the chaos as best they can. This sounds a bit dramatic, and thinking of your Main Street business as being enveloped in a fog of war may seem like an overstatement, but the concept is critical to your continued success. Reasonable people set the scene and let it play out, and as the environment shifts, their gut responses are based on their prior assumptions. But today's fast-changing world will typically present them with a scene that is anything but stable. The best things you can do are to gather as much information as possible as quickly as possible and to stay flexible. Creating long-range plans and working out the details of the future is nearly impossible, and unreasonable leaders don't try. Instead, they take action, measure and test continually, and make lots of adjustments.

Know What You Don't Know

Most people presume that they know more than they do. It's human nature. But believing that you know something when in fact you don't is dangerous. You'll make poor decisions, implement the wrong tactics, and—without timely feedback about your performance—follow those tactics down the road to ruin.

Unreasonable leaders embrace their own ignorance. You don't know what you don't know, yet, paradoxically, your job is to find out. Remaining open-minded is a start, but you have to go further by asking questions designed to understand a rapidly changing field when you're not even sure what part is changing. Having a strong set of control console indicators like the ones described earlier will help. Look for discrepancies, such as changes that are outside the norms or readouts that contradict each other. And *wonder why* a lot. Reasonable business owners fall back on their experience and explain the world based on that knowledge. Unreasonable entrepreneurs are willing to wonder why something happened and then conceive of alternative or discontinuous responses.

And never ever get wedded to your opening moves.

Stop Hunting for Causes and Do Something, Anything

Amelia is a sales consultant. She closes like a pro, but she was having a tough time finding new prospects interested in her products. I asked her what she was currently doing to find new interested parties. Surprisingly (or perhaps not so), she wasn't doing much of anything.

Her standard approach to finding new business was through word of mouth—that is, referrals. Word of mouth is a powerful client acquisition strategy, and many salespeople rely upon it. But if it's your only method, it can be way too unpredictable to be the sole source of your business.

I asked Amelia if she knew how her competitors found prospects. She wasn't really sure (most businesspeople have no idea what their competitors are *really* doing). Primarily through public speaking, she thought. And, of course, through direct mail and the Internet. Generic answers, but probably on the mark. I wondered why she wasn't speaking herself. Was she scared? She told me no, she was fine with public speaking; she had given talks in the past and had signed up several audience members as clients. The obvious question followed: why had she stopped?

She admitted that there was no real reason. Maybe it was inertia. Maybe it was that she didn't want to travel. Maybe she didn't know where to book the engagements. Maybe, maybe, maybe . . . She knew that speaking to groups could solve her new business problem; it had worked in the past, and it was working for others. But she just wasn't doing it. She wanted my help in figuring out why she wasn't doing what she "knew" she was supposed to do. She was willing to pay me for my services.

Given our society's beliefs, Amelia's desire for introspection seemed reasonable and appropriate. If you can get to the root cause of what's ailing you, we're told, then you can eliminate that cause and sail calmly toward your goal. There's even an entire discipline devoted to this kind of thinking. It's called, not surprisingly, *root cause analysis*. The thinking here is that if you have an unwanted situation that consumes time and energy, and it happens in a repeated fashion, then it might be a good idea to figure out what is really causing this situation so that it does not occur again. In other words, delve into the situation to find the real cause of the problem rather than simply continuing to deal with the symptoms.

The Myth of Root Cause

The concept of root cause is based on the principle that causes are linear—that one thing follows another, that underneath every problem situation is some other situation that is causing it, and that people are up to the task of figuring out what this is. This is pretty reasonable, and it would lead one to suppose that by digging deep enough, you can get to the heart of the matter, correct it, and voilà. Problem solved.

But the fact is that the world we live in is chaotic—which means that simple, subtle, and often undetectable things can result in big changes in other, seemingly unrelated things worlds away. This is referred to as the Butterfly Effect, which is based on a fanciful metaphor attributed to Austrian zoologist Konrad Lorenz. Lorenz at one point said that a butterfly flapping its wings in Brazil could set off a tornado in Texas. Chaos theorists label this, with characteristic aplomb, "sensitive dependence on initial conditions."

Complicating the problem further is that in many, perhaps most, situations, causation is not linear. There is not necessarily one thing that causes another, which in turn causes another; instead, there are often several or many overlapping causes influencing one another and conspiring to deliver the ultimate outcome. In almost any business situation worthy of consideration, the complexity increases to the point where understanding is impossible and ignorance inevitable.

Of course, rather than admit ignorance, we seize upon a likely causal candidate, call it the root cause, and declare victory. Until the next time the problem pops up, and we find ourselves once again on a root cause snipe hunt. Very reasonable, indeed.

Dismiss Psychology

In people, the myth that there is always a root cause has its, well, roots in Freudian psychology and all its derivatives. The idea that people's deviant actions can be explained by some failed sexual relationship or past traumatic experience makes us believe that if we can only figure out how we got this way, we can repair the problem, and it will never come back.

But this is like suggesting that the real reason that salespeople don't sell is that they *fear rejection* or that the real reason that a brilliant product manager keeps saying foolish things that scuttle deals is that she *fears success*. Anthropologist Gregory Bateson called things like "fear of success" an *explanatory principle*. It's a label that gives us a neat way to refer to something but that explains nothing and gives us no opportunities for effective action. Freud's explanatory factor (the root cause) doesn't explain anything. This approach doesn't work.

It may seem unreasonable to dismiss psychology, but sometimes that's what you should do. Knowing more about why you are the way you are rarely leads to doing anything about it, and it doesn't make you more inclined to go in a more productive direction. Werner Erhardt said it best, "Understanding is the booby prize."

So while on the surface it might be tough to argue with the idea of "finding the real cause," this approach is more suited to fixing problems such as repeated flat tires on your bicycle or quality defects in complex machinery than to figuring out why Johnnie can't read or, in this case, why Amelia can't sell. Root cause analysis is not that helpful when considering performance in human beings, and it is definitely not helpful for getting things done.

But root cause analysis—or any brand of excessive introspection—is an excellent way to avoid action. People tend to use the search for causes as busywork. They convince themselves that they're actually doing something worthwhile when what they're really doing is spinning their wheels. All this activity doesn't move the picture forward.

But back to Amelia. I wouldn't indulge her; I wouldn't be polite and pretend that what she was doing was going to help. She thought I was being unreasonable (I was) because rather than hunt for causes, I asked her to cut to the chase. If she knew that speaking to groups would bring her new clients and make her (and her company) more money, I wanted to know what she could do to get started, and when. Tangible stuff.

Once I shook her out of her lethargy, Amelia jumped in. She had lots of ideas, including ones about a new speech she could write and companies she could target as audiences for it. We used her ideas and created a game plan; we made measures, timelines, and clear accountabilities for each aspect of the plan. We put her into our tracking system.

Now, she has a plan with specific actions that she's committed to. She is acting on the plan and booking speaking "gigs." Will she succeed? It's too soon to tell, but the early indications are that she's out there connecting with many more people than with her "word of mouth" system. She's giving talks and getting some new business. And here's the thing: Amelia has upped her chances for success. A lot. And that's the best she can do. That's all you can do.

Root cause analysis has its place, especially in large, complex organizations, engineering environments, and manufacturing situations. And if you're an individual with a long history of repeated mistakes, then you probably should go in for this type of psychotherapy. But if you find yourself wasting a lot of time on trying to figure things out, stop it.

You're hurting yourself. Your mind will go around and around your subject, and it may never find the proper answer. If you aren't producing much and you suspect that you're in a cycle of near-endless rumination, here's a solution for you.

Do Something—Anything

Rather than trying to figure out why the situation is the way it is, take action. Of course you'd like your actions to be as effective as possible, but to get started, almost any action will do. The Nike people enshrined the phrase "just do it," and it sums up our whole philosophy. Stop thinking about why a thing isn't right, and do something that will change it.

So often we know what to do, but we don't do it because we think that what we have isn't just right or that there might be a better way.

People get stuck trying to think the perfect thought and create the perfect solution. Instead of acting, instead of putting the idea into production, they tweak it a little here, change a little there. They want to make things better, bit by bit. They're always polishing. Someday they may decide to launch; their great thought or solution will be ready for its grand debut. (Don't hold your breath.)

Perfectionism kills marketplace opportunity. No one knows this better than Bill Gates. What do you think all those differently numbered, differently named versions of Microsoft Windows we've seen over the years mean? They mean that Gates isn't a perfectionist, he's a realist. Microsoft has some of the very best minds in software programming available. It drives them until they come up with something that is good enough for the market, and then it releases what these people have created, warts and all.

Last I checked, Bill Gates was worth $80 billion—more than any other person on the planet. He doesn't sit in endless rumination. He doesn't polish, polish, polish until he's produced a thing of beauty. He gets his product out so that he can make money.

The entire software industry is run this way, and while many people moan and groan about all the bugs that software has, most would rather have the new product with bugs than the previous version without. At least that's how it seems with all those software sales.

Several years ago, I conducted a small study asking corporate software buyers whether, if they had to choose one or the other, they would rather have a product that was perfect, complete in all its stated features, but shipped late (perhaps very late), or a product that was less complete but could do the job and was shipped on time. The survey respondents came out very strongly in favor of having something that did the job in their hot little hands rather than having to wait.

Excellence or Perfection

> *A good plan violently executed now is better than a perfect plan next week.*
>
> —General George S. Patton

Conventional business wisdom suggests that things should be complete in every way and without any defects. In other words, we think that our things should be perfect. Unreasonable people have a much more productive idea. They contrast this idea of flawless perfection with the idea of making something that is of the highest quality or superior. In other words, unreasonable people look for excellence.

Perfect is when all the details are just so, with everything fitting into its place and every aspect being exactly as it is supposed to be. Excellence happens when the thing does its job in a superior way. Conventional business leaders seek perfection. Unreasonable business leaders seek excellence.

Perfection takes a long time to achieve, whereas excellence is a state of mind that can be reached quite quickly. They say the devil is in the details, and this often means that the details are the hardest part of any project and take the longest to execute. The unreasonable path to success questions the essential assumptions about which details are actually important and wonders whether you even know. While perfection may be something worthy to strive for, it does not always add to the final product.

The law of diminishing returns, originally applied to economics by Thomas Malthus, tells us that adding more details may not always bring with it a measurable increase in value or utility. One has to question how much better the shave is from Gillette Company's five-bladed Fusion razor. Does having five blades really make it superior? Is it really that much better than the four-bladed version, or the one with three blades? It may not be fair to examine product examples that are really marketing gimmicks, but perfectionism tends to have us always seeking for *more*, when what we really need is things that work well.

Perfectionists fritter away large amounts of time and money trying to get their ideas just right, whether the idea is for a product, a process, a book, or a new ball game. They are always trying to figure out whether something can be made better than it is instead of asking whether what they have will do the job well. Some writers can sit for hours "wordsmithing" a single sentence, while mystery writer Elmore Leonard writes a new novel from start to finish in 30 days. Unreasonable as it may seem, Leonard is one of the most productive and highest-paid writers today, and he has been for quite some time. People like his product the way it is—they get what they asked for, and they get a lot of it. Filmmaker Terrence Malick has directed only 4 feature films in his 30-plus-year career, and while he is considered by some to be a great artist, he hasn't made much money for the studios. Contrast this with director-producer Ridley Scott, who has created 18 films and made fortunes for himself and his backers.

Many marketers will work on a direct mail letter endlessly, changing the headline, or the opening, or the bullets, or the offer. But they never once bother to find out if anyone will buy the product, something that they could easily do by putting stamps on some copies of the letter and dropping them off at the post office.

Which do you think will work better? Trying to figure it out in the confines of your own office, or sending the letter to some prospects and watching to see if they buy something? Of course the latter, and yet many business owners think it is reasonable to spend tons of time getting things right. Successful direct marketers give getting a communications piece right their best shot, and then they test it by mailing a bunch and tracking the results.

What works is to bring your creation to the point where it looks like it will work well, and testing it in the marketplace. No one cares if your speech is perfect; they want the message. While some people will undoubtedly object to a malapropism or a misplaced modifier, others will hardly notice. And while some people will complain about the bugs in your software or a defect in your product, others—if it works as advertised in a superior way—won't really care.

There's another aspect to this issue of perfection, which is that many of our business concerns (at least the ones that matter) are way too complicated to get perfect. Remember the issue of complexity that we discussed earlier in this chapter? There are too many interactions and too many individual components for you to know with any degree of confidence which little bits are going to make the biggest difference. This means that the best you can do is strive to get it working, whatever "it" is, and then test it out in the real world. What is the customer going to say?

Whether we're talking about a product, a process, a speech, a letter, a book, or a new design for some thingamabob or whozi-whatz, rather than focus on perfection, simply try to get it ready for prime time. Show it to the world, and let the market's feedback continue the process. If it works and meets your standards for excellence, you've got it made, and you've saved a ton of time in the process. If your creation doesn't quite make the grade, fix the things that are wrong and bring it out again. Your public will be more than happy to tell you what it wants, if only you'll give it a chance.

The trick is to do something. You have an idea? Great. Get Version 1.0 up and running and get it into the marketplace. You'll hear about what's good and what's bad about it. Version 2.0 will be better.

Do the unreasonable: stop hunting for causes, don't worry about the explanation of why whatever is wrong is wrong. Just make it right. Get busy. Start producing, even if what you produce isn't perfect. You can always fix it later, and your people—whoever they are—are willing to help.

Just Don't

No chapter on execution would be complete without a section on what *not* to do. Being unreasonable means that you're going to do things differently from the way they're usually done; here is a list of common behaviors you'll want to avoid.

- Don't stay off track for more than one cycle. Getting off track is inevitable. Hold regular and frequent meetings to evaluate project status. The time between meetings is one cycle. Develop the will to close any gaps within the next cycle.

- Don't berate your team for being off track. Work to develop solutions that will get them back on track.
- Don't stay stuck. Even superstar performers lose their momentum and find themselves at a loss for what to do. They just don't stay stuck for very long. Losers view their stuckness as a problem, whereas the winners on your team see it as a momentary condition. The difference between success and failure is getting unstuck fast.
- Don't punish anyone in public. Better yet, don't punish anyone at all. Make sure all your people understand what's at stake, have a concern for the outcome, and see themselves as part of the solution. If someone doesn't, fire that person. He or she won't be happy with you anyway.
- Don't pad your delivery schedule to make sure you can win. Eliminate the "margin of safety." These are not life-or-death situations, and safety is really about covering your backside. Instead, estimate your real requirements based on the best information available, and do your best to make it so.
- Don't get distracted. Your team—whether it is your entire company or a small work group—has a mission to fulfill. Make sure that everything its members work on is in the service of that mission. When chronic interruptions and diversions arise, stop to find out if they are actually part of your mission. If so, include them in your execution plan. If not, do whatever you must to stop responding to them.
- Don't wait for a complete solution. It's important to comprehend the complete execution path so that you know you can "get there from here." That doesn't mean that you have to know every detail of subsequent phases of the solution before you go to work on the current one.

Dwight had a software development team composed of the top experts in his company. The team was on a crash project to create the next version of the company's software. After repeatedly missing deadlines, the company had made some very big promises to the customer base, and its future depended on on-time delivery. There were many technical problems to surmount, but the team dispatched them one by one. What it couldn't deal with were the constant interruptions from the Support and Service Group. Because the members of the development team were the experts, the support people kept turning to them to help whenever major client problems arose. This hampered the development managers' progress, and the project was in jeopardy. The chronic interruptions were actually a response to the company's great service mandate, and all proposed solutions seemed doomed. At an all-hands meeting, Dwight's team came up with an unreasonable solution. It completely detached the development group from the rest of the company. Its mandate no longer included support of any kind. To address support, two of the expert team members were transferred to the help group as go-to guys. The rest of the group was moved across town to its own offices, and all contact was cut off. The two groups didn't even share a phone switchboard. While this caused problems reintegrating the team with the rest of the company nine months later, the product was delivered, and the customer base was satisfied.

Just Do

The biggest barriers to execution are lack of communication, lack of involvement by senior leaders and planners in the execution phase, and lack of corporate will and discipline. The unreasonable execution solution starts by creating a culture of accountability and building upon that to develop the company's will to succeed. Build an atmosphere where people "can do," and use shared accountability to keep them doing it. Set aggressive timelines and do whatever it takes to remain within the tolerances of your schedule. Establish regular meetings and other systems of communication to clear away obstacles and reward progress.

EPILOGUE

We have tremendous potential for good or ill. How we choose to use that
power is up to us; but first we must choose to use it. We're told every day,
"You can't change the world." But the world is changing every day.
The only question is . . . who's doing it? You or somebody else?
Will you choose to lead, or be led by others?

—J. Michael Straczynski, creator and
executive producer of *Babylon 5*

It could happen 20 years from now or it could happen in 50, but
it will happen. Many people are deeply frightened by the idea.
Some think that it will add spice to our lives and make things
more interesting. Still others believe that it will make people
more like gods. What most people don't realize is that it will
mark the beginning of the end of humans as we know ourselves.
Is this sheer lunacy? Sheer fantasy? It may be unreasonable, but
it is neither lunacy nor fantasy. And the more you think about it,
the more you'll realize that as far as the future goes, this forecast
could prove quite accurate.

The singularity.

The what?

The singularity—the singular moment in time when computers develop the ability to program themselves, very accurately
and very quickly. The singular moment in time when everything
you believe about what makes people human changes beyond

recognition. The moment in time when human intelligence is superseded by superhuman machine intelligence. Remember what Bill Gates said about underestimating the long term? Thinking like Bill Gates, it is difficult to underestimate the impact that this event will have on everything we know about living on Earth. On the positive side, we—our race, that is—could have equal partners for the first time in our existence, if you leave out dogs. On the negative side, we could end up being the dogs.

If this sounds like Skynet from the 1984 movie *The Terminator*, you've got it just right. Except that this is not science fiction. This is a cold-blooded, clear-headed extrapolation from existing trends into the not-too-distant future. According to computer scientist and writer Vernor Vinge, it is quite likely to happen in the first half of this century. It works like this: when computers gain the ability to write their own software, they will also gain the ability to take control of all the electronica and mechanica to which they are connected. In other words, computers will be able to run the world—without us.

◆   ◆   ◆

Imagine that you are driving your car to work. No, scratch that.

Imagine that your car is driving you to work. You've told it your destination and the time you'd like to arrive, and that you prefer the scenic route. And that's it. Your car plans the route; negotiates with the GPS, the traffic monitoring system, and the other cars on the road; it does all the stopping, starting, and turning. You, on the other hand, read the morning's news on your tablet computer. You could have your tablet read to you if you preferred, but you still enjoy reading.

A call comes in from the colleague you were to meet, and a rather lifelike 3-D projection displays her in the passenger seat. She can't make it in person. Instead, she is sending a three-dimensional avatar—you'll hold the meeting by virtualphone. You might have done the same; many people do nowadays. But you're old-fashioned. You still like to smell flesh and blood. You like to feel someone's hand when you shake it. Everyone has quirks.

Does this future seem more reasonable to you than the singularity? This is one you could have figured out for yourself. Do you think there's something you could profit from?

◆　◆　◆

Or what if most of the diseases we know of are eliminated prior to birth, and the ones that are left—largely in people who were born before 2020—are treatable with gene therapy and protein-modulating drugs. People still die of "old age," only that isn't the biblical threescore and ten but a more Moses-like 120 years. Moreover, government-mandated population controls limit families to 1.7 children—you have to demonstrate exceptional circumstances to get a variance—and so most of the people you see are . . . well, they're old. And so are you.

You've already had three different careers. You're thinking about what to do next. Retirement? That's something only the underprivileged do. Anyone with sufficient resources creates his own "job opportunity" and continues to be useful. In this society, that's the mark of success.

You still play golf with those huge-headed nanotube-fiber drivers. You still go out to the movies; it's much more fun than staying at home—only, of course, they're not projected on a screen anymore. You still travel the world physically. After all, recreation and leisure are the fastest-growing industries on the planet. And off! You just don't do it all the time. The rich show off by working.

◆　◆　◆

What if you were sure that these things would happen? What if you believed that the trends were in place right now, and that the changes just described were already under way? Could you take advantage of them in some way? Could you turn them to your benefit? Is there a business to develop or a defensive move you would make?

None of these scenarios is far-fetched. You might not want to believe one story or another, but each of them is a likely extension of what is happening in the world today, in the very early years of the twenty-first century. Each of these circumstances is something that any businessperson could figure out on her own by reading the tea leaves in the cup in front of her.

We've talked throughout this book about unreasonable strategy, unreasonable tactics, unreasonable thinking, and unreasonable execution. This is the unreasonable future.

The main reason (sorry, but I had to use the word) for being unreasonable is to shift your company and quickly transform it from where you are at this very moment into something extraordinary. You now have the tools and the mind patterns to do just that, and there's nothing stopping you. There is a second reason (there's that word again). Remember the words of Alan Kay: "The best way to predict the future is to invent it." And the best way to invent the future is by unleashing your company from the shackles of reasonableness.

I don't know if the scenarios described here will become our future or not. To me, each of them seems quite likely, and it may be a matter of when and not if. Regardless of whether these plots play themselves out or something a bit more similar to what we know happens, you will be ready. Use these ideas, and you can be among the ones who make it happen. Talk about producing extraordinary results.

Please, take these tools and have at it.

UNREASONABLE
SUMMARIZED

Unreasonable is a must if you want to be extraordinary.

Unreasonable is ignoring conventional wisdom.

Unreasonable is going the distance.

Unreasonable is doing more than you are asked for. Much more.

Unreasonable is asking for more than people are usually willing to give.

Unreasonable is giving your best in every situation where your best is called for.

Unreasonable is not accepting compromise as a matter of course.

Unreasonable is about saying yes to yourself every time someone says no to your idea.

Unreasonable is acting on the possibility of great things, without worrying about the probability of success.

Unreasonable increases the probabilities of success by making sure that possible things become real.

Unreasonable is about making improbable, but much needed, things happen.

Unreasonable is questioning why the things that are considered normal are considered normal, and then figuring out how they really should be.

Unreasonable is about thinking thoughts without editing them so as to be reasonable.

Unreasonable is expecting the best, every time

Unreasonable is expecting success.

Unreasonable is expecting greatness.

Unreasonable is questioning why and why not.

Unreasonable is being totally responsible for the outcome.

Unreasonable is being irresponsible about transgressing accepted norms.

Unreasonable is asking, "Why should I?" every time someone says, "Be reasonable."

UNREASONABLE QUESTIONS AND ANSWERS

Q. Is being unreasonable like "thinking outside the box"?

A. No. Being unreasonable is not about thinking "outside the box" or outside anything else. As soon as you frame your thinking as "outside the box," you are thinking in relation to the box, which means that your ideas stem from how that box was structured in the first place.

Reasonable people base their future actions on the experiences that have been successful in the past— "the box." While that is generally a pretty good model, it ultimately runs out of gas, especially when the world to which that box was adapted is experiencing rapid or discontinuous change. Being unreasonable is about *not* being bound by the standard models on which you have been raised, and being willing to generate ideas and actions that do not fit the patterns on which you've built previous success. You may incorporate bits and pieces of your previous models or your industry's models or society's models, but then again, you may not. You are free to invent from scratch and free to try anything you please.

Another way to look at this is to first accept the existence of the box—"after all most people are thinking inside of it, so it must be there, right?" Next, you realize that the box just is, and it simply doesn't matter. The box is self-imposed. Take the box away. Now, what's left?

Q. Well, what about creative thinking? Is unreasonable thinking like that?

A. Creative thinking by itself is still about searching for creative solutions within the confines of the accepted wisdom of your industry. Creative thinking has a place in being unreasonable; it's just not the only thing. After all, it isn't really creative to say to someone, "What is your best?" and then ask her to produce a 15 percent greater result than whatever she said. It isn't creative at all, but it is unreasonable. And, believe me, it works.

Q. Does being unreasonable mean being confrontational?

A. Not by definition. There's nothing inherent in being unreasonable that means that you become more confrontational. However, as you pursue unreasonable strategies and tactics, and as you resist pressure to accept less-than-stellar approaches to your business, you may raise the hackles of the people you work with, thereby causing them to become more confrontational toward you. This is a natural outcome of your no longer suffering the status quo. One of the key reasons the norm became "the norm" in the first place is people's natural unwillingness to confront mediocrity. By being unreasonable, you are reversing years of acquiescence. So while being unreasonable doesn't mean that you will become more confrontational, you will most likely be involved in more confrontations. This, by the way, is one of the key reasons that people resist the very idea of being unreasonable. They would rather "go along to get along," as the saying goes.

Q. How do you see being unreasonable immediately benefiting executives?

A. There are several immediate ways in which being unreasonable will benefit executives and business owners.

The first is that executives need to think beyond the bounds of what is considered—in their industry—normal, proper, and even appropriate. When I work as an *unreasonable* growth consultant, one of the first things prospective clients say is, "But you're not from our industry." My response is, "Someone from your industry is the last thing you need. Your industry is awash with people who think like everyone else in your industry, *all thinking similar and perhaps overused ideas*. What is needed is thinking that is not bounded by the traditional logic of your industry, ideas that can bring a nonreasoning perspective."

The second immediate benefit comes from eliminating the reasons why things can't happen. Reasonable people think that there are *reasons why* things are the way they are, that there are *reasons why* we must do things a certain way, and there are *reasons why* certain approaches to business are going to work and others will not. They think that all these *reasons* are hard and fast, cut and dried. Being unreasonable causes executives to challenge the reasons why. Whenever someone starts to give me a *reason why*, I am moved to being unreasonable. I ask people to set those reasons why aside—to ask, "Well, what if we did? What would happen then? Would that work?" These questions open up the possibility that those *reasons* are no longer appropriate and meaningful, if they ever were.

The third immediate benefit is to eliminate excuses. When an executive—particularly a middle manager— doesn't produce the desired results, he often supplies a reason why his approach didn't work. So what you have is either desired results or reasons why not. Now, people act as if those reasons are almost as good as the results. How do I know this? Because people always say something like, "Well, it didn't work, but here's why not." Or, worse still, "We didn't get it done" or "We didn't even try." Stuff like that.

Being unreasonable takes away business leaders' option of resorting to reasons why not. I want to take away people's option of resorting to excuses. I think the whole of industry would shift if there were no "excuse" option—if all you could do was produce the desired result, or another way to get the desired result, or another way, and so on.

The fourth, immediate benefit is to set higher, unreasonable expectations. There's a story about an experiment in which teachers were told that tests showed that their students were below-average learners. The teachers appropriately lowered their expectations and taught at a lower level, and the result was less learning. They were then given an additional class whose "test scores" indicated above-average abilities. The teachers raised their expectations and taught at a higher level. The students again met the teachers' expectations, this time outperforming the norms. In both cases, the classes were within the norms; it was only the teachers' expectations that varied.

Business leaders will benefit dramatically by setting unreasonable expectations for their people. Use those unreasonable expectations as big, giant stakes in the ground—and then let your team figure out how to deliver and turn those unreasonable expectations into reality. Taking this approach with people, campaigns, initiatives, or projects is the surest way to dramatically increase the effectiveness and productivity of any business. Why should you settle—why should your customers settle—for what is reasonable and predictable? Why settle for the norm? Apply unreasonable thinking. Set unreasonable expectations. Demand unreasonable results.

**Q. How do you know how much to ask of people?
    When is it too much?**

A.   There is a powerful notion tied to the art of unreasonable requests. This approach will help every executive when working with vendors, contractors, and employees. Keep asking for more. Keep asking for better. Whatever is offered, up the ante. Ask people to perform beyond what *they* consider their best. And to do it sooner than they say they can. And with higher quality. And with greater effectiveness and lower costs.

This is not a negotiating tactic. It is not the same as what negotiators call "nibbling." It is simply asking people to perform beyond their own sense and beyond your sense of what is reasonable. Sometimes, even often, you will get that level of results if you ask for it.

Q. **What is the most common problem that executives can overcome to make their business planning more original?**

A. The issue is not to make planning more original per se; the issue is to implement business strategies that produce great results. Planning is often based on trying to achieve results that are "reasonable" given an organization's past history. Most businesses forecast their results, their revenues, their growth rates, and so on based on previous year's results. The norm is to call this approach reasonable, and most companies build their plans to realize these "normal" results.

Being unreasonable brings an attitude that begins with more useful planning questions: "What would make a profound difference?" "What would cause a transformation in this company?" "What would *dramatically* increase shareholder value or profits?" Discarding normal or reasonable goals and instead setting plans to achieve your company's vision gives you an immediate opportunity to leapfrog the *norm*ative state of affairs.

Five hundred years ago, when the Franciscan monk Luca Pacioli first codified double-entry accounting, the world changed very slowly, and an extrapolation of history was a rational approach. Even 200, or 100 years ago, basing your forecasts on the previous year's state of affairs made sense. But in the twenty-first century, change is rapid, sudden, and often overwhelming. This change is happening not only in our own business, but in your industry, the global economy, your customers' expectations, your workforce, technology, and all aspects of our shared culture. To think that anything from as long as a year ago will remain steady this year isn't just unreasonable, it's totally ridiculous.

Take *all* the factors into account. Bring *everything* you know about your specific situation up to date, add into it all the future changes that must be predicted, and add to that the purposes for which your company exists. The forecasted results might seem unreasonable, but there is no other way to go.

Q. Where is the line between unreasonable and ridiculous? What keeps people from crossing that line and jeopardizing their corporate identity?

A.   Fear of jeopardizing one's corporate identity is perhaps the biggest obstacle to creating breakthrough results. Most people are simply too concerned with looking good to take important risks. (Some people call this keeping your butt covered.)

We've said earlier that the only way to do anything significant is to take those risks. The only way to create giant breakthrough results is to create ideas and programs that are unreasonable and just go for it. I'm not sure there is a clear line between unreasonable and ridiculous that can be drawn beforehand. The line gets drawn in the aftermath. If you succeed, wow! If you fail, people will, with 20/20 hindsight, call your idea ridiculous.

Let's be clear: *unreasonable does not mean unthinking; it does not mean irrational.* There are mechanisms at work, and unreasonable thinking is about exploring and pushing the envelope and cross-pollinating and intuitive inventing.

But it is definitely not about not thinking. It may be that the line separating unreasonable from ridiculous ideas is where thinking has been left behind, or perhaps where there is no thinking at all.

Q.   How do you hope to affect the business world with the introduction of this *unreasonable* idea?

A.   Being unreasonable is, well, unreasonable. My hope is to create a group—a large group—of business owners and executives who are willing to champion bold, counterintuitive, and unreasonable ideas leading to breakthrough thinking, breakthrough projects, and breakthrough results. The outcome for the business world will be a richly diverse sea change, a massive generator of profitable and productive ideas that companies could tap.

On a global level, there are many problems that are not yielding to tried-and-true reasonable approaches and techniques. Unequal distribution of global well-being is one such issue. The world's energy dependence on fossil fuels is another. My hope is that a self-organizing network of unreasonable thinkers might get some traction on these problems.

Q.   Do you use this idea in your own work? How has it benefited you so far?

A.   Our whole approach is unreasonable. We call ourselves Business Accelerators. We promise Quantum Growth. By "quantum" we mean discontinuous and nonlinear jumps in performance. These are already unreasonable things, since most people don't think the idea of quantum anything in the macro world is reasonable. We've systemized our consulting process—work that most people consider idiosyncratic and intuitive—and built a reliable machine for transforming businesses consistently and quickly.

We begin our work with unreasonable premises and strive for breakthrough results. Then, and only then, do we figure out how to execute them. We insist on its being fun, and we insist on its being profitable. We expect people to commit to results, and we have a low tolerance for excuses or reasons why they don't achieve them—although we do expect them to learn and grow, no matter what the outcome. Along the way we continually make unreasonable requests of our people, demanding and—I hope—causing them to be their best.

INDEX

ABOUT THE AUTHOR

Paul Lemberg is "The Unreasonable Consultant," who helps clients see the unnecessary limits they place upon themselves and then gets them to take bold and at times uncomfortable actions that lead to reaching their dream goals. Through the years Paul has worked with leaders at Accenture, Adobe, American Skandia, Cisco Systems, Goldman Sachs, IBM, JPMorgan Chase, Lexis/Nexis, OpenText, and SAIC, and thousands of smaller entrepreneurial and emerging companies.

Paul is Chief Business Accelerator and CEO of Quantum Growth Consulting, an international consulting firm that helps entrepreneurs and executives rapidly create More Profits and More Life™. He is the author of two other books and hundreds of widely published management, marketing, and leadership articles. His monthly executive e-letter, *Extraordinary Results*, is read by over 20,000 business leaders.

Paul lives in California with his wife, Leslie, and their two children.

Visit Paul on the Web at www.paullemberg.com.